D1002527

The Gospel According to Genesis

A GUIDE TO UNDERSTANDING GENESIS 1–11

by
Charles C. Cochrane

WILLIAM B. EERDMANS PUBLISHING COMPANY
GRAND RAPIDS, MICHIGAN

To Isobel,
Donald, William, and Douglas

Library of Congress Cataloging in Publication Data

Cochrane, Charles C., 1910-
  The Gospel according to Genesis.

  Includes bibliographical references.
  1. Bible. O.T. Genesis I-XII—Criticism,
Interpretation, etc. I. Title.
BS1235.2.C63 1984   222'.1106   84-4047
ISBN 0-8028-1971-0

Contents

Acknowledgments

In the preparation of this modest volume I have been greatly assisted by the wholehearted encouragement, valuable suggestions, and helpful criticisms of Dr. Robert Lennox, formerly Principal and Professor of Old Testament Literature and Exegesis, Presbyterian College, Montreal, now retired; and Dr. Arthur C. Cochrane, recently Professor of Theology at Pittsburgh Theological Seminary, and presently Special Lecturer in Ecumenical Theology at Wartburg Lutheran Seminary, Dubuque, Iowa. In thus acknowledging my indebtedness to them I do so without committing them to the views expressed and the interpretations offered in these pages, for which I alone am responsible.

I am no less grateful to Dr. Joseph C. McLelland, Dean of the Faculty of Religious Studies, McGill University, Montreal, for his consenting to provide a foreword to these chapters.

CHARLES C. COCHRANE
Waterloo, Ontario
Canada

Foreword

The beginning of the Bible sets the stage not only for the story to follow but for all sorts of problems too. Since the debate over creationism *versus* evolution continues to plague this Continent, it is timely to have a book offering a fresh approach to Genesis 1–11. It is fresh in insisting on taking "gospel" as horizon and pattern, so that the material under discussion may strike us with its power in introducing the Good News. The choice of "parable" to denote this literary genre is no doubt debatable, as are many of the author's judgments in trying to understand and to explain the complex of stories, genealogies, problems of space and time, and generally dense text he has chosen for his subject. But that is to be expected and welcomed, rather than the simplistic way or the dogmatic manner in which these chapters are usually approached. It is to Dr. Cochrane's credit that he does not sidestep thorny problems nor fall into the trap of offering a "final" answer for every difficult question. Would that more preachers and teachers of the church were so modest in their claims and diligent in their research!

For these reasons it is my pleasure to introduce a book aimed at helping us appreciate the worth of that part of Scripture which is perhaps too familiar, and so too easily misinterpreted. To discover gospel in these ancient texts is a gain for both our understanding of these chapters in Genesis and our grasp of gospel.

JOSEPH C. McLELLAND, *Dean*
Faculty of Religious Studies
McGill University

Introduction

For a period of some fifteen years it was my immensely rewarding privilege to teach a course in Christian education to the students of Westmount High School in Montreal, Canada.* As a minister with a full range of pastoral responsibilities I had neither teacher training nor previous teaching experience. Accordingly, there was much to learn about teenagers, about classroom procedures, and about teacher-student relationships. In addition, it seemed essential to speak to students' major concerns, difficulties, and areas of doubt. What subject matter, I wondered, would best serve this purpose?

To find an answer, I listened carefully to their questions for nearly three years—as those questions arose in class. It was simply a matter of allowing the students to teach the teacher what to teach. As the questions poured in, it became overwhelmingly apparent that the Book of Genesis, especially the first eleven chapters, posed the greatest difficulty. This is readily understandable if for no other reason than the students' early exposure to the study of various branches of modern science which are widely believed to contradict the teachings of Genesis. In the current absence of any positive direction to the contrary it is almost inevitable that young people should find the early chapters of the Bible "unreliable" as a vehicle of truth.

---

*Readers in the United States are reminded that in the province of Quebec the elementary and secondary school systems are organized and administered according to confessional (Roman Catholic and Protestant) rather than secular (public and private) preferences. Consequently, the vexing question of religion in the schools does not normally arise.

If the matter were to end there, the situation would perhaps not be so serious. But such is not the case. Doubt feeds on doubt, generating and reinforcing an attitude of skepticism toward the whole of the Old Testament, and extending to the New Testament as well. No greater calamity could befall either the young people or the church. This situation is not eased by the presence in our school systems of many teachers who, though they be ever so competent in their own fields, have little or no appreciation of the nature of the biblical material.

But why, we wonder, do these young people have the greatest difficulty with the Book of Genesis? They might have been expected to ask about the virgin birth or about the resurrection of Jesus as matters of first concern in a course on Christian education. But those questions came later—and almost incidentally—in discussion periods. The chief area of interest was graphically illustrated by a question raised in class: "Sir, what is the relation between Adam and neolithic man?"

This study of the early chapters of Genesis is intended for all those who are interested in the narrative of God's first dealings with mankind, including young people. When one is old enough to ask a question, he or she is old enough to receive an answer. My own experience has led me to believe that some of the brightest minds in any community are to be found in the secondary schools.

The material presented in this volume is an expansion and deepening of that originally offered to the young people in the classroom. In making it available to a wider community, I have avoided, as far as has been possible, any reference to the technical questions which must arise for the specialist. The purpose is the same here as it was in the classroom: to provide guidance to all those who are seeking to come to grips with the rich foundations of Christian faith in the narratives of early Genesis.

CHAPTER ONE

Our Father Abraham

The story the Bible tells really begins with the opening verses of Genesis 12: "Now the LORD said to Abram, 'Go from your country and your kindred and your father's house to the land that I will show you. And I will make of you a great nation, and I will bless you, and make your name great, so that you will be a blessing. I will bless those who bless you, and him who curses you I will curse; and by you all the families of the earth will bless themselves.' "* Or, "in thee shall all families of the earth be blessed" (KJV).

These words give expression to what the church recognizes as God's covenant with Abraham, or the call of God to Abraham. The whole message and theme of the Bible springs from and depends upon this promise of God. It is the foundation of his majestic plan for the salvation of mankind. In this encounter God has chosen one man, from whom he will create an entire people. They will be his servants in the enterprise which he is about to undertake for the whole world. This people whom God will create in the calling of Abraham (for Abram/Abraham, see Gen. 17:5) will be the bearers of the blessing which will be extended to include all the families of the earth.

Abraham was the eldest of the three sons of Terah. Terah may have belonged to an ancient tribe of seminomadic people, the 'Apiru, of Mesopotamia. We are told that all three sons were born in Ur (Gen. 11:28), a city of the Chaldeans located near the mouth of the Euphrates River (present-day Iraq). The

---

*Unless otherwise indicated, all Scripture quotation is from the Revised Standard Version (RSV).

youngest son, Haran (the father of Lot), died at Ur before the migration of the family began. The original destination seems to have been the land of Canaan (Gen. 11:31), but on arriving at Haran (a bit more than half the distance) the family decided to stay. During their sojourn in Haran, Terah died, leaving Abraham as the patriarch of this little band of travellers.

The dates of Abraham's migrations cannot be firmly fixed. It is believed, however, that they took place not much earlier than 1900 B.C., and certainly not later than 1750 B.C. Both the biblical sources and recent archaeological findings support this estimate.

It is important for us to recognize at the outset that there is nothing in the record of Genesis to suggest that Abraham was in any respect an exceptional person—at least, nothing prior to his encounter with God. There is no suggestion that he had earned this distinction. We are told nothing of his having qualities of heart and mind which might, perhaps, entitle him to be selected as a servant of God. Indeed, elsewhere in Scripture there is a hint to the contrary. On one occasion Joshua began an address to the tribes of Israel as follows: "Thus says the LORD, the God of Israel, 'Your fathers lived of old beyond the Euphrates, Terah, the father of Abraham and of Nahor; and they served other gods' " (Josh. 24:2). Joshua is forcefully reminding his people that God's calling of Abraham, and their own status as the people of God, was an act of sheer grace on God's part. Much, much later the apostle Paul would use the same circumstance to say the same thing about the church. Neither Abraham nor Israel nor the Christian *earns* or *merits* God's favor; the preeminence of all three is quite undeserved. It is a work of mercy which, through Abraham and Israel, God wishes to bestow on all mankind. What Abraham did do was to believe God's word and trust in him. Accordingly, Paul quotes from Genesis 15:6: "Abraham believed God, and it was reckoned to him as righteousness" (Rom. 4:3). This means that if you and I follow Abraham's example in accepting the gospel, it will be reckoned to us as righteousness, too. This is how we understand "in thee all families of the earth [have been and] shall be blessed" (KJV).

When we look closely at the terms of God's covenant with Abraham, it appears that this arrangement leaves much to be desired. The promise itself is firm enough, surely, but its content is obscure to the point of vagueness. Abraham is required to abandon his familiar surroundings in Haran and simply "go." Where? To an unknown, unnamed land. It could have been a mountain, a plain, a desert, a valley, or an island. From him will come a great nation. What kind of nation? A nation great in peace, or great in war? Great in numbers, or great in wealth? No details are given. Abraham will be blessed—with no indication of the nature of that blessing. His name will be "great," but whether in statesmanship, military prowess, wisdom, or personal charm is not stated. God will, however, show favor to Abraham, and he will bring hardship upon those who inflict hardship on him. One concrete aspect of God's promise is that he will defend and protect his servant, come what may. And, finally, that elusive word *blessing,* a blessing which will embrace all families (peoples, races, nations) of the earth. All this is summed up in the vivid words of the writer of the Letter to the Hebrews: "By faith Abraham obeyed . . . and he went out, not knowing where he was to go" (Heb. 11:8).

The terms of the covenant are repeated several times, in whole or in part, in the Book of Genesis (15:5; 17:4–8; 18:18–19; 26:4; 28:13–15; 32:12; 46:3), but they are never changed and are never made more explicit. For the most part these repetitions take the form of reassurance—first to Abraham, then in turn to Isaac and Jacob, as the heirs of the promise.

How are we to understand God's presenting a covenant to Abraham without "spelling out" the details, except in the broadest possible terms? What God had in store for Abraham was utterly priceless. We know that now, but Abraham could not have known it at the time. If God had revealed his plan to Abram in the fulness of its detail—its inducements, its rewards, and its tremendous scope—he might well have been tempted to obey *for those reasons*. He may have obeyed because it was to his material advantage to do so. That is not what God required of Abraham, and it is not what he asks of us. He wants us to believe and obey him for his own sake, simply because he is our Father and loves us dearly. The rewards will come, and our lives will be infinitely richer for our having obeyed. But we are not to obey for that reason. Abraham was being asked to place his life in God's hands and at his disposal, unconditionally. The same is required of us. (There is a striking similarity between Abraham's response to God's call and that of the disciples to Jesus' invitation as recorded in Matthew 4:18ff. Jesus summoned, and the disciples followed.)

That God should choose a single, obscure, and almost solitary figure such as Abraham; that in doing so he created a new people distinct from all others; that, shepherded by a succession of leaders—prophets and priests, judges and kings—this people should eventually achieve the status of nationhood with its capital at Jerusalem; that through almost twenty centuries of recurring victory and defeat, prosperity and famine, voluntary exile and involuntary captivity, this nation was preserved—all of this is a story worth telling. It is drama on a grand scale. And when we see the final act played out in the birth, life, death, resurrection, and ascension of Jesus Christ we are able to grasp, in some measure at least, the height, depth, and breadth of God's love for his children. It is little wonder that Paul considered himself called upon "to preach to the Gentiles the unsearchable riches of Christ, and to make all men see what is the plan of the mystery hidden for ages in God who created all things" (Eph. 3:8–9). This plan, which is the theme of the Bible in all its parts, is commonly spoken of as God's covenant of grace, or the drama of salvation.

If God's call to Abraham means what we believe it does, and if it is to have far-reaching effects on all mankind, and if God's intention is that of "blessing," and if the nature of that blessing may properly be described as salvation, then there is an element we are not yet aware of. Something is missing. Why did it appear to God that his creature needed salvation—needed to be saved? Saved from what? Rescued for what?

Although the *story* of the Bible begins in Genesis 12, that is not where *the Bible* begins. It begins with what we now recognize as a prologue, a preparatory statement, so that we may be informed and equipped to understand the story that follows. The truth is that if we had no knowledge of the first eleven chapters of Genesis we could not possibly know why God called Abraham. It is therefore to the prologue, Genesis 1–11, that we now direct our attention. We will return to Abraham and his family in the concluding chapter.

4

CHAPTER TWO

The Nature and Meaning of Creation

In the early chapters of Genesis* we encounter a strange, singular kind of literature; there is no other quite like it. It speaks of matters pertaining to a time long before the dawn of recorded history. It tells of God's incomparable act of creation to which, in the nature of the case, there could be no witnesses. Accordingly, there is no possibility of creation having been observed and later recorded. In the prologue we read of situations and incidents—and their consequences—of which we could have no knowledge drawn from observation, reason, or experience.

This material, then, is not history as we normally understand that word, though it does have its roots in history. It is rather *pre*history. This insight need not undermine our confidence in the value of the prologue for an understanding of our faith. When we know what it means we will be better able to estimate its importance—and not until then.

It must be emphasized as strongly as possible that the writers of the early chapters of Genesis were not attempting to give a scientific account of the origin of the universe. Just as these stories originated before the age of recorded history, so also they were told prior to the development of the natural sciences. Indeed, if we read the first two chapters carefully, and listen intently to what is written, we will realize that nothing is said about *how* God created the heavens and the earth. We are simply told that he did it: God spoke, and it was done. Creation is presented to us as an act of God's will. How it was

*The word means: start, beginning, origin.

5

done is God's secret, and it appears likely to remain so. There is a hint of this in the second chapter, where we are told that prior to the creation of the woman "the LORD God caused a deep sleep to fall upon the man" (Gen. 2:21), and when the man awoke she was there. This may suggest that man is not to be a witness, then or now, to God's creative act.

As we allow our minds to dwell on the biblical teaching about creation, what we are being told becomes increasingly clear: God created the heavens and the earth out of nothing. Indeed, although the word *create* is used quite frequently in conversation today, in the Bible its Hebrew equivalent is used only of God. So Paul in his Letter to the Romans writes of the God who "calls into existence the things which do not exist" (Rom. 4:17). And the writer of the Letter to the Hebrews teaches that "by faith we understand that the world was created by the word of God, so that what is seen was made out of things which do not appear" (Heb. 11:3).

It was not the case, then, that God took material which was "at hand" and out of that material made, constructed, molded, or formed the universe. No; he called it into being. He gave it existence. At this point we have reached the outermost limits of our ability to see and visualize. Bonhoeffer states: "For we cannot speak of the beginning; where the beginning begins our thinking stops, it comes to an end. . . . In thinking of the beginning, thinking collapses."[1] An understanding of *how* things began and came into existence is denied us on every hand. We can only see the results of the operation. That something comes out of nothing is utterly unimaginable and indescribable. It is God's miracle, and God's secret.

In view of the fact that no satisfactory answer to the question of the origin of the universe has yet been found, and with the very real possibility that it never will, it is curious that men persist in the search. In the early seventeenth century an Irish bishop, James Ussher, widely known for his scholarship, confidently announced that the universe was created in the year 4004 B.C. He even gave the date and the hour! It is for that reason that many of the older copies of the Bible, at the top of the first and following pages, carry that date. It is also reported that more recently a Russian mathematician calculated the distance from earth to God as nine light-years (that is, the distance travelled in nine years at the speed of light). His method for determining this was quite simple. After the Russians were defeated by the Japanese in 1905, it took nine years for the Russian prayers to reach heaven, and nine more years until they were answered by an earthquake that hit Japan in 1923!

Modern scientists are considerably more modest and less confident than their predecessors were. As often happens, the greater the advancement in human knowledge, the greater our awareness of our ignorance. Two contrasting theories of the origin of the universe are in the forefront today. One points to the slow evolution of hydrogen atoms over a period of five and one half billion years; in the other view, a "cosmic explosion" took place some four and one half billion years ago, giving rise to the cosmos as we know it today. Regarding the first of these suggestions the scientists who advance it at the same time acknowledge, "With our theory the mystery of creation is as great as ever."[2] Proponents of the other view are similarly self-effacing. In *The First Three Minutes*, Steven Weinberg admits, "We cannot deny a feeling of unreality in writing about the first three minutes as if we really know what we are talking about."[3]

In this question of the origin of the universe, there is no reason for natural scientists and biblical scholars to be in dispute, for in point of fact they are not talking about the same thing. Science speaks of things that were and are, and of the changes that have taken place since things came into existence millions (billions?) of years ago—development and regression, growth and decay, survival and extinction. It tells of upheavals in the earth's surface, ice-age glaciers, magnetic fields, variations in climatic conditions, and changes in the courses of rivers and levels of water. It tells us, then, how the world has been formed and molded by the forces of nature since its inception. But science can tell us nothing about the primal *origin* of the universe, though it frequently (and mistakenly) uses that word. The Bible, on the other hand, is speaking about *existence*—yours and mine, and that of the world and the universe. It does not give us a theory; it confesses a faith. It proclaims that the existence of the cosmos—in its entirety—is the gracious work of a divine Creator, and that it is therefore intentional, deliberate, and purposive. It did not just "happen."

Faith in God the Creator is not peculiar to the Book of Genesis. As even a random sampling of passages from both the Old Testament and the New will show, it is the faith of the Bible—and therefore of the Christian church. Ezra extols his God in the following manner: "Thou art the LORD, thou alone; thou hast made heaven, the heaven of heavens, with all their host, and the earth and all that is on it, the seas and all that is in them; and thou preservest all of them" (Neh. 9:6). At one point in the dialogue between them, God questions Job: "Where were you when I laid the foundation of the earth?" (Job 38:4). The psalmist raises his song of praise: "When I look at thy heavens, the work of thy fingers, the moon and the stars which thou hast established; what is man that thou art mindful of him, and the son of man that thou dost care for him?" (Ps. 8:3–4). Isaiah joins the chorus: "Thus says the LORD, your Redeemer, who formed you from the womb: I am the LORD, who made all things, who stretched out the heavens alone, who spread out the earth" (Isa. 44:24). And: "Thus says the LORD: 'Heaven is my throne and the earth is my footstool; what is the house which you would build for me, and what is the place of my rest? All these things my hand has made, and so all these things are mine,' says the LORD" (Isa. 66:1–2).

In keeping with the fuller revelation of God given in Jesus Christ, the New Testament references to God and to the Creator provide greater detail. John writes: "In the beginning was the Word, and the Word was with God, and the Word was God. He was in the beginning with God; all things were made through him, and without him was not anything made that was made" (John 1:1–3). And: "He was in the world, and the world was made through him" (John 1:10). He who was the Word of God "became flesh and dwelt among us" (John 1:14), that is, Jesus Christ. John is saying that in the beginning Christ was already there. Walter Luthi comments: "He was active as creator and redeemer long before the world became aware of it, for Christ is older than the knowledge we men have of him."[4] Referring to his existence prior to his human birth, Jesus once said, "Before Abraham was, I am" (John 8:58).

This theme, the participation of Christ in the miracle of creation, is repeated and enlarged on throughout the New Testament. "The God who made the world and everything in it, being Lord of heaven and earth . . . himself gives to all men life and breath and everything" (Acts 17:24–25). Of God the Son (that is, Jesus Christ), Paul wrote to the Colossians that "in him all things were created, in heaven and on earth, visible and invisible . . . all things were created through him and for him" (Col. 1:16). In the Letter to the Hebrews we read that "in these last days [God] has spoken to us by a Son, whom he appointed the heir of all things, through whom also he created the world" (Heb. 1:2). And later, using language similar to that of John's Gospel, the author of Hebrews writes: "By faith we understand that the world was created by the word of God" (Heb. 11:3). It is in this way that we may speak of God the Father as the Author of creation and of God the Son as its Agent.

From these passages it is evident that according to the Bible the concept of creation is all-inclusive; it embraces the sum of reality apart from God. Everything that is not God, that is distinct from God, owes its existence to his creative act—from the lowly flea that pesters the family dog to the galaxies of outer space. Since God has made the whole of creation, he is also the creator of mankind. In addition to owing its *original* existence to God, every created thing is also utterly dependent on his sustaining grace and power for its *continuing* existence. The Creator is present to his creation. He has not abandoned it, turned it over to someone else, or left it to get along by itself, for "he himself gives to all men life and breath and everything" (Acts 17:25). In short, I would not be writing this, and you would not be reading it, if God did not give to both of us life and breath to do so.

In a curious turn of events, what God has created at times accounts for "belief in God." There are many people who say, "Of course I believe in God! There is no other way to explain what we see around us. How else could we account for the seasons, the foliage, the fertility of the land, the world in which we live, the sun, the moon, and the stars in their courses? No one in his right mind would deny the existence of God!" (Perhaps so; but there are many who do!) However well-intentioned such grounds for believing in God may be, they have little in common with biblical teaching. As D. T. Niles observes:

9

Throughout the ages men have sought to prove the existence of God. They begin their argument from something they know directly and show that the argument leads inevitably to Him. The world is, therefore there is a Creator. There is a design in the world, therefore there is a Designer. Things are, and therefore there is a ground of existence. There is a moral world, and therefore there is its Guarantor. . . . Something other than God is more certain, more immediately known, more directly experienced and on this other the belief in God is based. But the Bible begins with God. God is, therefore there is a world. God is, and therefore there is a purpose in life. God is, and therefore things are. God is, and therefore there is law and also grace. Nowhere in the Bible is there an attempt to prove the existence of God.[5]

Men and women who claim to believe in God because they have no other way to account for the world of nature really do not know him at all. God is not a conclusion that we draw from the fact that the world exists. (There are other conclusions we might draw, and which might be equally plausible.) If that were true, God would be nothing more than our explanation of something else—of the fact that the world exists. He would then be the product of our human minds; or, worse still, a figment of our imaginations. He would have no reality independent of our conception of him, no existence other than that which we attribute to him. If that were the case, *we* would be *his* creators!

The biblical teaching is just the reverse of this. The Bible *begins* with God, and only then do we learn that he called Abraham, formed Israel, sustained the prophets, sent his Son, and gathers the church. "In the beginning *God.* . . ." The God who is spoken of (and who speaks) in the Bible is self-existent, owing his existence to nothing and to no one. He is the eternal reality; he is not an inference we can draw from something else, or something prior, or about whom we can inform ourselves. It is he who has created all things, and upon whom all things depend. He is (now), and was (before the world began), and ever shall be (world without end).

We have said that the creation stories—and the prologue itself—are not history as we know it, and that they are not scientific as we have come to understand the practice of science. Then what are they? They are a statement of faith *in narrative form*. They cannot be understood in any other way.

They acknowledge, accept, and proclaim the news of God's revelation (disclosure of himself) as Creator of all that was, is, and is to come. This, no less than the gospel of Jesus Christ, is God's word to all mankind, for he is the one God and Father of us all. To say that we believe in God the Creator because that is what the Bible teaches is neither ignorance nor religious arrogance. It is simply a statement by which we recognize that the Bible is, in all its parts, the word of our God, and that his word is to be trusted and believed as it speaks of him. The New Testament, for example, does not teach a doctrine of creation different from that of the Old. Indeed, having read what the New Testament has to say about creation we are able to understand what God has done in creation more clearly than if we had read only the Genesis passages. As one writer has put it, "What is said in prospect of Him [God] can be understood only in retrospect of Him." And by this we mean that what is said of God in the Old Testament anticipates what is said of him in the New, and can be fully understood only in the light of the New (that is, in the light of the gospel of Jesus Christ his Son).

The knowledge that God created the heavens and the earth has enormous practical consequences for our understanding of God, man, and the world. This knowledge tells us a great deal about *God,* for not only do we know that the universe and its inhabitants did not just "happen," nor is it the work of some identified or unidentified "power," or the result of mere chance, but we know it to be the work of a *Person*—whom we have learned to call "Father." This fundamental conviction that the Creator of the ends of the earth is our Father means that we need "fear no evil; for thou art with me" (Ps. 23:4). That is, you and I need never fear that we have been abandoned and are at the mercy of whim or blind chance, for "even the hairs of your head are all numbered. Fear not, therefore; you are of more value than many sparrows" (Matt. 10:30–31).

The doctrine of creation also tells us who *we* are; and in an age of recurring identity crisis—not only among the young— this is crucial. When Jeremiah received the call to prophesy, he discovered that God knew more about him than he had ever dreamed. "Before I formed you in the womb I knew you, and before you were born I consecrated you" (Jer. 1:5). You and

11

I can be the son or daughter of Mr. and Mrs. Smith, or Jones, or Cochrane; but that is not all we are, for the Smiths and Joneses and Cochranes are themselves *children of God*. It is quite wrong to say, as many confused people are saying today, "I belong to myself. What I do with my life is nobody's business but my own!" Even after we have entered adulthood, and we may no longer be said to belong to our parents, we remain God's children by virtue of both our creation and our redemption. "You are not your own; you were bought with a price" (1 Cor. 6:19–20; see also 7:23).

Finally, the knowledge that God is our Creator profoundly affects our thinking about the *world*. We know that the world is not eternal; it is finite. It came into being and continues to exist only at God's good pleasure. It has no life of its own apart from and independent of God. Paul's words, "in him we live and move and have our being" (Acts 17:28), can be applied to all of creation, as well as to mankind. If we and all creation did not live and move and have our being in God, we and the world would have no existence at all. It is clear that this is the teaching of the New Testament, for we read, "Heaven and earth shall pass away" (Matt. 24:35; Mark 13:31; Luke 21:33). It is perhaps for this reason that Jesus warned the multitude: "Do not lay up for yourselves treasures on earth, where moth and rust consume, and where thieves break in and steal" (Matt. 6:19). And again, "The form of this world is passing away" (1 Cor. 7:31; see also 2 Pet. 3:10; 1 John 2:17). It is unwise for us to place our final confidence in what this world has to offer, because your destiny and mine is "an inheritance which is imperishable, undefiled, and unfading, kept in heaven for [us]" (1 Pet. 1:4).

In closing this study of the nature and meaning of creation, we consider the question, *Why* did God create the heavens and the earth? What was (and is) God's reason and purpose in his creation? Why did he bring into existence a person, made in his own image—so to speak, an "other"? In seeking an answer to this all-important question we begin by noting again that the creation does not exist by itself, but by the will of God. The presence of created things is not self-explanatory. Similarly, the *reason* for the presence of created things is not self-evident. Accordingly, the aim, objective, and purpose of creation is not to be sought in creation itself, but only in the God who made it, maintains it, and cares for it. Apart from God, the world and the universe have no goal, no purpose, and no destiny—and life itself is quite without meaning.

According to the Bible it is quite impossible to understand God's creative act except as the work of his overflowing love. From all eternity he loves the world he has created, and longs to demonstrate his love for it. This becomes clearer and more explicit as we continue in our reading of the Scriptures. God earnestly desires to have an "other" with whom he can enjoy fellowship, and with whom he can enter into partnership. Creation may therefore be understood as the sphere, the arena, the place where this relationship is established, and where God's quite incomprehensible love is displayed and demonstrated. It is the "theatre" of God's glory: "The heavens are telling the glory of God; and the firmament proclaims his handiwork. Day to day pours forth speech, and night to night declares knowledge. There is no speech, nor are there words; their voice is not heard; yet their voice goes out through all the earth, and their words to the end of the world" (Ps. 19:1–4).

The sequel to the act of creation is the covenant, the "partnership" into which God freely enters with his creation. It is the covenant which declares, proclaims, and reveals the meaning of and the reason for creation—namely, God's desire for fellowship with beings made in his image. Apart from the covenant we would be hard-pressed to discover a reason for our own existence, and that of the world around us. Perhaps that is why many people of our generation are looking in vain for meaning and purpose in their own lives. They are looking in all the wrong places. Of course, it is possible to accept substitutes for the meaning which God has given to our lives; but it is not profitable for us to do so. To pursue wealth, pleasure, and status—as though they were capable of giving meaning to our lives—is an illusion. They may come; and if they do we may be grateful for them, yet realizing all the while that they are the sort of things that perish while they are being used.

If creation is the *work* of God's love, the covenant is the *expression* of it. The covenant is God's assurance to all his creatures that his love for us is a genuinely historical, visible reality—now and always.

CHAPTER THREE

The Question of Truth

Many readers of the Bible find themselves wondering about the "truth" of the stories in the early chapters of Genesis. "How *reliable* are the narratives?" they ask. Many of them, especially young people, mean "Did this happen?" Is it a fact that there was a serpent in the Garden of Eden who spoke and was spoken to? Is it the case that God actually walked in the garden in the cool of the day? And what are we to make of the statement that Adam and Eve, suddenly realizing that they were wearing no clothing, sewed fig leaves together to cover their nakedness?

In seeking answers to these questions we may note first of all that there are many areas of life and experience in which truth may be sought—of which history is only one. As an example of *historical* truth, consider the following sentence: "The armies of the Duke of Wellington and the emperor Napoleon fought the battle of Waterloo." That statement is true because this did indeed occur in the early years of the nineteenth century. A second example: "It is wrong for me to steal from the neighborhood supermarket." This, again, is a true statement; but it is hardly historical. I have never stolen from the neighborhood supermarket. But the statement is true, nevertheless. We call it *moral* truth. Or again: "7694258753 $\times$ 82685419738 = x" (x being the product when the two numbers are multiplied together). In this equation x is always a constant; that is, no matter how many times these two numbers are multiplied together, the correct answer is always the same. It is possible, of course, that these two numbers have never been multiplied together, but the statement is nevertheless true. We call this *mathematical* truth.

Finally, let us consider the proposition "God loves mankind." We believe this to be a true statement. It is not, properly speaking, historical (though there is plenty of historical evidence for it). We call this religious or *spiritual* truth; and in doing so we offer the following definition: *religious or spiritual truth is truth concerning the relationship between God and mankind.* It is this truth with which the Bible is principally concerned.

It is the function of a prologue, whether of a book (when it is usually called a preface or a foreword) or a play, to "set the stage," to introduce the main characters, to tell of the relationships of the characters to one another, and, in general, to fill in the background. In this way the reader or audience will more readily grasp the theme of what is unfolding before them. The first eleven chapters of Genesis perform this indispensable function by means of six stories which form not only a series (that is, following one after another) but a sequence (that is, each story is related to the previous narratives, and each is dependent on the others for its contribution to the whole).

These stories are referred to by some writers as "myth" or "saga." Occasionally the word *legend* is used. However, there is not enough agreement on the precise meanings of these terms to warrant their use in a book of this kind. (The popular understanding of "myth," for example, is that it is a story that is not true and has no connection with truth; whereas the academic or classical meaning is very far from that.) For reasons of clarity and simplicity, the present writer prefers the word *parable.* We are already familiar with this word from Jesus' frequent use of parables as a method of teaching his disciples and the people of his time. Surely no one would accuse Jesus of being false because he told the story of the Good Samaritan or the parable of the Prodigal Son. Accordingly, we offer a second definition: *A parable is truth conveyed and expressed in story form.*

It cannot be emphasized too strongly that in these early chapters of Genesis we are dealing with serious and important matters. It has been said that two of the best-known and best-remembered stories are those of Adam and Eve, and Cain and

15

Abel—and that may very well be true. In John Steinbeck's novel *East of Eden,* three of the characters become involved in a discussion of these stories. One of them, Lee, says, "No story has power, nor will it last, unless we feel in ourselves that it is true and *true of us.* . . . If the story is not about the hearer he will not listen. . . . I think this is the best-known story in the world because it is everybody's story. I think it is the symbol story of the human soul." [Italics mine.] Another writer has put the same conviction in these words: "Adam becomes historical with every human birth." It is this kind of truth to which the stories of early Genesis attest. They are not fiction, fables, or fairy tales; they are *truth.* Genesis speaks of a real creation, of real disobedience, and of a genuine separation between God and mankind. Man's tragic disobedience to God is not something that happened once for all a long time ago. It is true in every moment of existence. For the truth about you and me is twofold: we are separated from the God who made us; and it was not God's intention that this should be.

There are really only two characters in the Bible—God and mankind, the Creator and the creature. The prologue introduces them, sketches the background which led up to the calling of Abraham, and prepares us for the larger story the Bible is about to relate.

CHAPTER FOUR

A Parable of Creation by the God Who Is High and Lifted Up

1:1 *In the beginning God created the heavens and the earth.* With these words the story of God's creative activity begins. The words form a sentence and make a general all-embracing statement about the origin of the universe in which we live. When we look closely, it becomes apparent that this is also a caption or heading—a kind of title, and that it tells us in the broadest possible terms what we will learn in detail in the verses that follow. An alternative reading, given in the footnote (RSV)—"When God began to create the heavens and the earth"—tends to confirm this observation: verse 1 is both a statement in its own right and a heading for what follows.

1:2 *The earth was without form and void, and darkness was upon the face of the deep; and the Spirit of God was moving over the face of the waters.* Biblical scholars are agreed that verse 2 is one of the most difficult verses in the Bible to understand, and, in addition, that a proper interpretation of it is crucial to an understanding of creation itself. What *is* this that is "without form and void"? And what is the meaning of the "darkness . . . upon the face of the deep" over which the Spirit of God was moving? This problem is by no means new. For example, the great St. Augustine (354–430 A.D.) suggested no fewer than five ways in which this verse may be understood. And every scholar since his time has also had to come to terms with what is written here.

Certain it is that verse 2 stands in sharpest contrast to the verse that precedes it, and to those that follow. Of what is

17

verse 2 a description? Many answers, in addition to that of St. Augustine, have been given to this question. Some have thought that this verse describes "material" created by God from which he (later) formed the heavens and the earth. Others explain it as a reference to a primeval reality which—whether created by God or not—preceded the act of creation, and which is accordingly independent of creation and outside the sphere of God's creative activity.

Surely, neither of these explanations does justice to the intent of Scripture. With regard to the first, there is simply no indication in the words of the text of the existence of any material prior to the onset of God's creative activity described in Genesis 1. Similarly, there is no scriptural warrant for affirming a primeval reality which may be said to precede the act of creation. Such an assertion would flatly deny the biblical statement that God created the heavens and the earth *in the beginning*.

Accordingly, we must look further for a proper understanding of verse 2. The Hebrew words which are rendered "without form and void" in our English Bible are used elsewhere in Scripture to convey the sense of "wilderness," "emptiness," "vacuum," "gulf," "abyss," "chaos," and "vanity." (This is the same pattern followed in the Septuagint, the early Greek translation of the Old Testament.) These words in verse 2 are also used to describe the idols of heathen nations, and those who design and worship them. And, finally, they are sometimes used in referring to a statement which is empty of meaning and content—a vain utterance.

It has been suggested that the second clause in this verse, "and darkness was upon the face of the deep," is a complementary view of the desolation described in the first clause, and superimposed on it. According to this interpretation, what God faced at the moment of creation was—Nothing. Quite literally, Nothing: nonexistence, nonbeing. The author of these words is trying to describe what is essentially indescribable; hence our difficulty in understanding this verse. As Bonhoeffer spoke of the collapse of our thinking when we attempt to comprehend the beginning of all things (chapter 2), in the same way it is quite impossible for us to think of, or visualize, Nothing, for we have no experience of it. We can only point to it by the use of negative concepts such as formlessness, emptiness, vanity, vacuum, gulf, abyss, vacuity, void, and chaos. Bonhoeffer comments: "The void . . . is thus not the matter of which the world has then paradoxically come into being. . . . The void is absolutely nothing."[1] It is mentioned only because God has overcome it.

In God's majestic act of creation he has rejected, repudiated, and denied the Nothing—that is, nonexistence. He has turned his back on the shambles described in verse 2. He has contradicted the darkness; he has chosen being in preference to nonbeing; he has opted for life rather than death.

1:3 – 4 *And God said.* . . . This simple clause is repeated ten times in the first chapter of Genesis, and on each occasion it is the expression of God's divine will. The world and the universe come into existence solely by being summoned to do so by God's creative word. The psalmist understood it perfectly: "By the word of the LORD the heavens were made, and all their host by the breath of his mouth. . . . He spoke and it came to be; he commanded, and it stood forth" (Ps. 33:6,9). In the New Testament we are told that this word became flesh in the man Jesus, and that "without him was not anything made that was made" (John 1:1ff.). It is in this sense that we may speak of God the Father as the Author of creation and of God the Son as its Agent (see chapter 2). It is important to notice that Jesus' word, during his earthly ministry, possessed much the same power. He "cast out . . . spirits with a word" (Matt. 8:16), and the centurion asked that Jesus "only say the word, and my servant will be healed" (Matt. 8:8). Probably the most vivid demonstration of the power of the creative word in the New Testament is in Jesus calling Lazarus from death and the grave (John 11:1–44).

"Let there be light."

Light is the first thing created. By that act of God, darkness stands rebuked. In the universe which will result from God's continued creative work, darkness shall not prevail. There is no mention of God having created darkness. Darkness is therefore to be understood negatively—as the absence of light, the opposite of light. It is known only in its separation from light, and because the light now shines.

1:5 *God called the light Day, and the darkness he called Night.* By giving names to the light and the darkness God asserts his sovereignty over both. "The darkness and the light are both alike to thee" (Ps. 139:12, KJV).

According to the first creation story, light was created before the sun, moon, and stars were formed: light on the first day, the sun, moon, and stars on the fourth. This statement is so at variance with the teaching of modern science that it calls for special comment. What was our author's purpose in setting forth the acts of creation in this order? We have already observed (chapter 2) that in the first two chapters of Genesis nothing is said about *how* God created the heavens and the earth; we are simply told that he did it. We have also said that the Bible is principally concerned with truth in the realm of the relationship between God and man—and not with issues of a scientific nature. Does the order in which the light and the sun appear in the first creation story mean that the author was mistaken, or that he did not know what he was doing? By no means; there is good reason for believing that what he did was done deliberately. By putting the creation of light before that of the sun our author may well have been giving the lie to the teaching of other religions, ancient and modern, that the sun is God, or a god. Karl Barth states: "This presentation is at this point an open protest against all and every kind of sun-worship, or the worship of other heavenly bodies."[2]

The sun, the moon, and the stars are created things, and all three have as their appointed function to "separate the day from the night," to "give light upon the earth," and to be "for signs and for seasons and for days and for years." To the sun and the moon the additional responsibility of "ruling" is assigned—the sun by day and the moon by night. These heavenly bodies are intended to serve as the measures of time and space—the clock and the compass—which will make it possible for the creature (man) to become aware of his place and time on earth, and so to participate in the life all around him. Although the sun and the moon are commissioned to rule over the light and the darkness, there is no mention of their having been appointed to rule over man. Accordingly, we may observe in passing that the fanciful notion, which is both ancient and curiously modern, that human life is influenced, governed, or

20

determined by the stars (astrology) is quite out of place and has no warrant in Scripture.*

"And there was evening and there was morning, one day."

It is evident that in creating the light as an alternative to darkness God also created time. We become aware of the existence of time through the fact that it *passes*: there is day and there is night, and there are seasons and years. Time, as an aspect of creation, is transient. The peculiar order defining the first and subsequent days, in which the evening is mentioned before the morning, corresponds to the Jewish custom according to which the sabbath (Saturday) begins at sundown on Friday evening.

In the church's pursuit of truth in the first chapter of Genesis a good deal of attention has been paid to the precise meaning to be attached to the word *day*. Are we to understand it to mean a twenty-four-hour day, a solar day, in spite of the sequence in which the creation of the sun, moon, and stars is recorded? Or is "day" intended to signify something else altogether—perhaps successive stages of God's creative activity? We are all familiar with the Bible's use of "day" for purposes other than to denote a twenty-four-hour interval: "For a thousand years in thy sight are but as yesterday when it is past, or as a watch in the night" (Ps. 90:4). "In that day, the branch of the LORD shall be beautiful and glorious" (Isa. 4:2). "Your father Abraham rejoiced that he was to see my day; he saw it and was glad" (John 8:56). Is the use of "day" in the first story of creation another such occasion, or do we have an obligation to accept it as referring to a twenty-four-hour interval?

A brief survey of the thinking of some of the truly great teachers of the church will suggest that there is no universally agreed answer to this question. For Origen of Alexandria, the problem here is not only the meaning of "day" but also the much wider concern of what the implications of a severely literal interpretation of Scripture at this point would be. He wrote: "Now what man of intelligence will believe that the first and the second and the third day, and evening and morning existed without the sun and moon and stars? And that the first

---

*For biblical injunctions against the practice and use of astrology, see Deuteronomy 4:19; 18:10–12; Isaiah 47:13; Jeremiah 8:2; 27:9; and Galatians 4:9.

day, *if we may so call it,* was even without a heaven?"[3] [Italics mine.] Clearly, Origen looked upon the use of "day" in this connection as a figure of speech.

In one of his best-known works, *The City of God,* St. Augustine writes concerning the days of creation, "Of what fashion those days were it is either exceeding hard or altogether impossible to think, much more to speak."[4] Augustine, too, had difficulty in assessing the meaning of "day" as used in the creation story.

In his commentary on Genesis John Calvin[5] betrays no interest in the subject, failing even to mention it. Accordingly, we are probably correct in assuming that he understood "day" in Genesis to refer to a twenty-four-hour period.

Martin Luther also makes no reference to the matter in his treatment of Genesis 1. Nevertheless, in commenting on 2:4b— "In the day that the LORD God made the earth and the heavens," he writes: " 'In the day' here is to be taken for an indefinite time, as if Moses has said, 'At that time.' "[6] In this comment we may detect a certain flexibility in Luther's understanding of the letter of Scripture, but it is much too brief a reference to warrant our drawing firm conclusions.

When we read modern-day theologians and commentators, we find a similar lack of unanimity among them. For Karl Barth it is absolutely essential to a proper understanding of the text to recognize the creation day as a twenty-four-hour period. Anything else is an "evasion." He insists that "the fact that God calls the light day means formally that the day as our unit of time is not an arbitrary human invention or convention, but a divine work and institution. The day is thus given to the creature as the sphere of its existence. . . . No one and nothing, not even the sun or any constellation, let alone man, has the right to withdraw from the day the purpose assigned to it by the consecration of light."[7]

Bonhoeffer sees the matter quite differently. "The physical problem does not at all belong to the discussion in which the 'day' is being considered. It does not disparage biblical thought, whether the creation occurred in rhythms of millions of years or single days, and we have no occasion to protest the latter or to doubt the former. . . . To the extent that his word is the word of man the biblical author was limited by his time and knowledge, and we dispute this as little as the fact that *through this word only* God is speaking to us of His creation."[8] [Italics mine.] In this statement Bonhoeffer is making a concession to the human element in the biblical record, where his illustrious contemporary refuses to allow it.

Among more recent commentators the same divergence of interpretation exists. Derek Kidner discusses the choices (including the literal twenty-four-hour concept) at some length, suggests reasons for the use of "day," and concludes: "A God who made no concessions to our ways of seeing and speaking would communicate to us no meaning." He adds, "It is only pedantry that would quarrel with terms that simplify in order to clarify."[9]

For Alan Richardson, "the 'days' of creation are to be understood as poetic symbols and not as definite periods of time, whether of twenty-four hours, or of a thousand years, or of a geological epoch."[10] Charles Fritsch takes the opposing view: "That the writer had in mind literal days in this chapter is made clear by the hallowing of the seventh day in 2:2–3. Therefore to interpret 'day' in these passages as a long period of a thousand years . . . or a geographical period is both unnecessary and incorrect."[11]

In the face of such a maze of conflicting scholarly opinion, to whom does the sincere student turn for help? Or, as Alexander Pope expressed it in his *Moral Essays,* "Who shall decide when doctors disagree?" Yet all is not lost. Surely no injury is done to the meaning of the narrative by accepting the word *day* in the literal sense. Similarly, it is no injustice to the biblical story to regard it as a vehicle to express, in a manner intelligible to the human intellect, the truth that the universe is God's creation. Perhaps this is why Bonhoeffer could write that "the question as such does not concern us."[12]

This brief excursion into the meaning of "day" in the creation story has been undertaken for two principal reasons. First, it is not unusual to find that many people, old and young alike, are disposed to reject and even to ridicule the biblical witness at this point as being primitive, naïve, and even quaint— and therefore quite unacceptable in the light of modern knowledge. Given this point of view, it is only one step further to conclude that since at the outset Scripture has been found to be either inadequate or inaccurate, or both, the Bible has very little to contribute to the life of mankind in the twentieth century. Nothing, of course, could be further from the truth.

Concerning the charge that Genesis 1 and 2 is an inadequate or inaccurate account, it must be said that man's fund of knowledge has never played the decisive part in the interpretation of Scripture. Origen and Augustine both lived centuries before the dawn of the age of science, yet both had serious reservations about the precise meaning to be attached to the word *day* in the creation stories. On the other hand, Barth and Fritsch, twentieth-century scholars, make no concessions to modern thought in their understanding of the same passage. It would therefore appear that whether we are convinced that creation days were solar days or that "day" signifies longer periods of time, our decision should be reached from sources within Scripture itself rather than from considerations of an external nature.

A second reason for pursuing the meaning of the word "day" is that this subject has given rise to great controversy and even to factions within the church. Those holding the view that a solar day is the correct interpretation at times derided and decried the views of others as being unfaithful to the letter of Scripture. Conversely, those who favor the longer or indefinite period have been known to pour scorn on those who hold to the solar day. Surely, all of this is as unnecessary as it is unfortunate; and it distracts attention from the essential teaching of Genesis 1: that God is the Creator of the ends of the earth— and of you and me.

1:6–8 *And God said.* . . . The story of creation, at regulated intervals, continues in all its majestic grandeur. We begin to sense, dimly at first, that what God is accomplishing here is of an essentially preparatory nature. There is just a suggestion, but no more than that, that great as these things are, greater things are yet to come. In these verses we meet what Bonhoeffer calls "the world of the fixed, the firm, the unchangeable, the unliving."[13] At God's bidding the "firmament" comes into existence. In ancient times the firmament (what we call the sky) was thought to be a dome-shaped vault supported by pillars at the ends or corners of the earth. In Amos 9:6 we read that the Lord, God of hosts, "builds his uppers chambers in the heavens, and founds his vault upon the earth." It was believed to be of solid construction, such as hammered metal. "Can you, like him, spread out the skies, hard as a molten mirror?" (Job 37:18) For the ancients, there were openings or windows in the firmament, whose function was to separate "the waters which were under the firmament from the waters which were above the firmament." When God opened the windows, the rains came!

1:9 – 13 *And God said. . . .* At this point God has separated the light from the darkness, and the waters from the waters. A further division was required: the waters under the heaven from the dry land. At a word from God this, too, was accomplished.

"And God saw that it was good."

That is to say, it was functional; but it was scarcely beautiful. Therefore, in the same "breath," God said: "Let the earth put forth vegetation. . . ." And so it was. The appearance of plants and trees of many kinds, each containing the seed which, under God, would assure their continuing reproduction, was the Creator's first act resulting in living organisms. This completed, the work of the third day was finished.

1:14 – 19 *And God said. . . .* See vv. 3–5 above.

1:20 – 23 *And God said. . . .* On the fifth day God did for the air and the water what he had done for the dry land on the third day: he filled them. In response to his word the waters "swarmed" with living creatures, and the air was filled with "every winged bird according to its kind." And all were blessed and received this invitation and command: "Be fruitful and multiply."

1:24 – 25 *And God said. . . .* God now calls forth creatures to inhabit the dry land. All is now in readiness. There is light and darkness, and the sun and the moon to rule over them. There is sea and dry land, trees and vegetation; there are living creatures in the waters, birds in the air, and animals and creeping things on the earth. All have been blessed and made fruitful in the functions allotted to them. *Then* God said, "Let us make man. . . ." That is to say, when all else was in place and functioning, God created man. According to Genesis 1, the first account of creation, the creation of man is not only the final act or stage in the creation sequence, it is also its purpose and goal. Everything that has gone before is of a preparatory nature, with the creation of man in view.

1:26 – 31 *Then God said, "Let us make man in our image, after our likeness. . . ." So God created man in his own image, in the image of God he created him; male and female he created them. . . .* At first reading, the use of the word *us* in this verse appears unusual, and even inaccurate. One would perhaps have expected to find some such statement as, "Then God said, 'I will now make man in my image, after *my* likeness.' " The use of "us" forbids the reader from thinking of God as alone and solitary. It suggests the presence of others, and a consultation among them resulting in a unanimous decision to create man.

Yet in verse 27 the *singular* is used: "So God created man in his own image, in the image of God he created him; male and female he created them." The selective, alternate use of the singular and plural forms in these sentences is remarkable. We are on delicate ground here: we dare not say more at this stage than is warranted by the text. Barth comments: "It [Genesis 1] is the first creation record which is either sufficiently naïve or instructed to regard God as capable of the soliloquy expressly narrated in the plural . . . and [which] felt it important to say so at this particular point in the creation of man."[14] At no time has the church understood this phrase as evidence of a plurality of gods, but rather as indicating a plurality *within God himself.* Within the Being of God himself there is a counterpart, a differentiation, a distinction to be recognized: an "I-Thou" relationship—notwithstanding the fact that God is one God.

In this connection it is important for our understanding of the first account of creation to know that the Hebrew word for "man," *adam,* is a collective noun. It is not the word for an individual person, but for the species, for humanity. The species itself is singular, even unique; therefore the singular noun is used. Yet within the singularity of the species there is also

26

a plurality, a differentiation, a distinction to be recognized—
an "I-Thou relationship to be discerned: male and female.

The image (and likeness) of God in which man is created is
not a quality in man, nor yet the sum of his qualities. There is
no biblical warrant for our seeking to identify the image of
God in terms of man's attitudes, attributes, traits, character-
istics, capabilities, or potentialities, however noble and praise-
worthy these may be, or be thought to be. The image and
likeness of God is what man *is*, by virtue of his having been
created by God to be his counterpart and partner. Man is created to correspond to God his Creator. He is a person as God
is Person. Accordingly, when God speaks to man he can and
does expect a reply—a response. What God and man have in
common by virtue of man's being created in God's image and
after his likeness is *personhood*. The relationship between the
Creator and the creature who is made in his image and likeness
is therefore "Person-to-person"; and man is in this relationship from his very beginning. This is what scholars know as
the "I-Thou" relationship.* For example: "*I* am the Lord your
God. . . . [*Thou* shalt] have no other gods before me" (Exod.
20:2–3). Or again, "On the day *I* called, *thou* didst answer
me . . ." (Ps. 138:3). The "I" and "Thou" are interchange-
able, depending on whether it is the Creator or the creature
who speaks.

Here, then, is God's true counterpart, one with whom he
can have conversation and community; one with whom God
is able to communicate, and who in turn can communicate
with God. For all of the fact that man is human and not divine,
he can truly be God's partner in a way that is neither given to
nor attainable by the rest of creation. No other object of God's
creative activity is said to be "in his image, after his likeness."

To this new and final creation, man, the Creator gives dominion "over the fish of the sea and over the birds of the air
and over every living thing that moves upon the earth" (v. 28).
Man has this, not as a possession but as a gift; not as of right,

---

*It should be noted that what has been called the "I-Thou" relationship be-
tween God and man is also the pattern or paradigm of God's relationship with
Israel in the covenant, of Christ's relationship with the church (his bride), and
of one individual to another, including that of husband and wife in the covenant
of marriage.

but as of grace. His lordship is therefore not divine and absolute, but creaturely and limited. The fish, birds, and every living thing do not belong to man, for "the earth is the LORD's and the fulness thereof, the world and those who dwell therein" (Ps. 24:1). But God has placed all these creatures in man's keeping. Man reigns on earth, but he reigns as a steward who is responsible to him who is Lord of all, including, of course, man himself. The pattern of creaturely lordship is based on the lordship of the Creator, from whom it derives. It is to be beneficent, gentle, and firm rather than tyrannical, despotic, and arbitrary.

Together with the appointment to lordship and the blessing of God come the invitation/command: "Be fruitful and multiply and fill the earth and subdue it" (v. 28), and the gifts: "I have given you every plant yielding seed which is upon the face of all the earth, and every tree with seed in its fruit; you shall have them for food" (v. 29). And looking back over all he had made, from the creation of light on the first day to the creation of man on the sixth, God saw that "it was very good." Not good as opposed to evil, for evil is as yet unknown; but good in the sense of pleasing (to God), satisfactory in terms of the purpose it is intended to serve, namely, as the theatre of his glory, the place and object of his love, and the scene of his covenant.

2:1–2 Thus the heavens and the earth were finished. . . . And he rested on the seventh day from all his work which he had done.   Since God saw the work he had done as "very good," there was no need for further work of a creative nature, and no room for improvement in what had been accomplished. Accordingly, he "rested," ceased from work, on the seventh day. Are we to understand that God was tired, even exhausted, by his labors and needed an interval in which to recuperate? It seems unlikely, especially in view of the words of the prophet Isaiah: "Have you not known? Have you not heard? The LORD is the everlasting God, the Creator of the ends of the earth. He does not faint or grow weary, his understanding is unsearchable" (Isa. 40:28). One writer likens God's rest from the work of creation to an enthronement in which the emphasis—but only the emphasis—passes from God as Creator of the uni-

28

verse to God as Lord of all he had created. In the same vein Kidner, citing Hebrews 8:1 and 10:12, compares God's rest on the seventh day with "the symbolism of Jesus 'seated' after His finished work of redemption [i.e., the new creation] to dispense its benefits."[15]

2:3 *So God blessed the seventh day and hallowed it. . . .* God's "work" of the seventh day, as distinct from that of the preceding six, consists of ensuring that the day will be fruitful in the role and purpose assigned to it; he blesses it. It is a day reserved for the celebration of the completion of his work of creation, in which he graciously invites the creature to join him. Therefore he "hallowed" it, declaring it to be a holy day to be "remembered" and "kept" (Exod. 20:8) in joyful thanksgiving for all that he had done. In consecrating the seventh day and thus setting it apart from the others, God requires of man no more than he himself is prepared to do, and did. He ceased to work. Man is neither commanded nor expected to work incessantly; he is not to become obsessed with, nor the prisoner of, his work. For man is more than the sum of his labors— he is the child of God. "If you turn back your foot from the sabbath, from doing your business* on my holy day . . . if you honor it, not going your own ways, or pursuing your own business . . . then you shall take delight in the LORD, and . . . I will feed you with the heritage of Jacob your father" (Isa. 58:13–14).

The purpose, for man as God's partner and counterpart, of the institution of the sabbath is that he shall be free (from work) to celebrate God's goodness and hear his word; so that ultimately he "might know that I, the LORD, sanctify [him]" (Ezek. 20:12; see also Exod. 31:13).**

---

*Preferring, in this instance, the footnote rather than the printed text (RSV).
**For a brief treatment of the relation of the Jewish sabbath to the Christian Lord's day, see my *Jesus of Nazareth in Word and Deed* (Grand Rapids: Eerdmans, 1979), pp. 78–80.

CHAPTER FIVE

A Parable of Creation by the God Who Is Near at Hand

One or two observations and comments of a general nature may help us understand the relationship between the first and second accounts of creation.

It is evident that the first story of creation "spills over" into the first three verses of Genesis 2, describing the events of the seventh day, and God's rest. Students of the Bible are divided on the question of where the second story of creation begins. Does it begin with verse 4a: "These are the generations of the heavens and the earth when they were created"? In this view, these words serve as an introduction to what follows. Or are these words intended to bring the first story to a close, summing up what has been narrated? In this interpretation, which seems to be the more likely, the second account of creation would begin in verse 4b: "In the day that the LORD God made the earth and the heavens."*

The God spoken of in the second chapter of Genesis is one and the same God who is proclaimed in the first. It is also the same creation and the same creature in both narratives. But the stories themselves are quite different. The most obvious

*In the early copies of the Bible, Old Testament and New, the text was not arranged in chapters and verses. The first complete translation of the Bible into the English language, the Wycliffe Bible (1384), was also the first to divide the material into chapters. The further division into verses came later, with Tyndale's translation (1534). Some rather arbitrary divisions result: see, for example, the twenty-first chapter of the Book of the Acts, which ends by *introducing* Paul's address to the Jews in Jerusalem. The present instance may be another example of this somewhat arbitrary division into chapter and verse.

30

difference is the order in which the creation takes place. In the first story, man is created last—after vegetation, birds, fish, and beasts; and woman is created at the same time as man. In the second story, man is created first, and afterwards the trees, the beasts, and the birds—and, finally, woman. Nevertheless, the purpose in both narratives is the same: to show the preeminence of mankind over all other created things. The first story does this by presenting the creation of man as the culmination (and crown) of God's work. The second achieves the same effect by placing him first in the order of creation.

There are other differences as well. The first story is told as though from above—as it were, from God's point of view. God himself never "puts in an appearance," if we may be permitted to express it that way. He is the Creator and Lord, and accordingly is hidden and remote—awesome and majestic in his power. Or, as Bonhoeffer aptly described it, "God in His deity." The second account portrays God as living (or at least appearing) on earth and in communication with man. He talks to and with his creature. Later we read of him "walking in the garden in the cool of the day." He is near, intimate, and solicitous for man's well-being.

Writers of both the Old and the New Testament testify to this dual aspect of God's relationship to the world: his remoteness (transcendence) and his nearness (immanence). We learn of God's transcendence in the following verses: "Behold, heaven and the highest heaven cannot contain thee; how much less this house which I have built! . . . Hear thou in heaven thy dwelling place; and when thou hearest, forgive" (1 Kings 8:27,30). "Truly, thou art a God who hidest thyself, O God of Israel, the Savior" (Isa. 45:15). And Paul writes to his co-worker Timothy about "the King of kings and Lord of lords, who alone has immortality and dwells in unapproachable light, whom no man has ever seen, or can see" (1 Tim. 6:16). On the other hand, we also read of God's immanence: "But thou art near, O LORD, and all thy commandments are true" (Ps. 119:151). "I know that I shall not be put to shame; he who vindicates me is near" (Isa. 50:7–8). And from Paul, "He is not far from each one of us, for in him we live and move and have our being" (Acts 17:27–28). As Alfred Lord Tennyson wrote:

> Speak to Him thou for He hears,
>   And Spirit with Spirit can meet—
> Closer is He than breathing, and
>   Nearer than hands and feet.

The presence in the Bible of two accounts of creation has led some scholars to assert that these stories have their origins in two quite distinct sources or traditions. It is almost inevitable that attempts should be made to reconcile or harmonize them; but it is doubtful whether this can be achieved without doing violence to the text of one or the other. The two accounts are portrayals of the same thing, but from two sides or points of view. It is probably wiser to read *both* stories, and let them contribute to our understanding, each in its own way.

2:4b *In the day that the LORD God made the earth and the heavens.*   From the first story of creation we have learned that "God" created the heavens and earth. For the Israelites, both before and after they entered the land of Canaan, the question arose, "Which God?" "Whose God?" Was it Molech (god of the Ammonites), Astarte (god of the Phoenicians and Canaanites), Baal, or one of the other gods of ancient times? The second story of creation seeks to pinpoint the identity of God the Creator in contradistinction to other gods. The Creator was the *Lord* God.

The Hebrew word *Yahweh* is used in verse 4b for the first time in Scripture, and it is translated "Lord." Since it is used in combination with another Hebrew word, *Elohim,* we read, "the Lord God." God is here telling his covenant people Israel, early in their history, that the God of creation is the same God who called and chose a people unto himself through Abraham. Accordingly, the Israelites never needed to be in doubt concerning the identity of God the Creator. Isaiah puts it most vividly: "For thus says the LORD, who created the heavens (he is God!), who formed the earth and made it (he established it; he did not create it a chaos, he formed it to be inhabited!): I am the LORD, and there is no other" (Isa. 45:18).

2:5 *When no plant of the field was yet in the earth and no herb of the field had yet sprung up. . . .*   The second account of creation begins in much the same way as the first—with God denying, rejecting, and rebuking barrenness and sterility, and opting for life. This verse corresponds to verse 2 of chapter 1.

2:7 *The LORD God formed man of dust from the ground, and breathed into his nostrils the breath of life; and man became a living being.* As in the first story, the Hebrew word for "man" is *adam,* which is derived from *adamah,* meaning "earth" or "soil." This is, again, the generic use of the word *man*—that is, mankind, or humanity. (The Hebrew for an individual male is *ish*; and for a female is *ishshah.*) Thus Adam is the man of the soil in a twofold sense: he is not only the tiller of the ground missing in verse 5b—the husbandman, but more particularly he himself is of the earth. He comes from the earth, he tills the earth, and he returns to the earth. "Behold, I have taken upon myself to speak to the Lord, I who am but dust and ashes" (Gen. 18:27). And, "These all look to thee. . . . When thou hidest thy face, they are dismayed; when thou takest away their breath, they die, and return to their dust" (Ps. 104:27–29). Accordingly, there is little basis here for pride. Humility would be more in keeping with our lowly, unpretentious origin. As verse 19 tells us, man shares his beginnings with the beasts and the birds.

Does this mean that man is simply another, even if special, form of animal life—perhaps the highest attained and attainable? Absolutely not; for God "breathed into his nostrils the breath of life; and man became a living soul" (KJV). Surely the King James Version is to be preferred here to that of the Revised Standard—"a living being"; and both of them to that of the New English Bible—"a living creature." All cattle and birds of the air and beasts of the field are living creatures, and may perhaps even be considered living beings; but no one would mistake one of them, a cow, for example, for a living *soul.* Of no other created thing is it said that God breathed into its nostrils the breath of life; and no other created thing can be said to be a living soul. According to the second story of creation, the uniqueness of the human species consists in the intimate divine ministration portrayed in verse 7.

2:8–17 *And the LORD God planted a garden in Eden, in the east; and there he put the man whom he had formed. . . .* Seeming

33

to choose his words with the utmost care, our narrator achieves the greatest clarity within a space of ten verses. Here is a word picture of what a loving Creator has done for his creature. He planted a "garden" (the Hebrew word can be translated "park" or "park land") in "Eden" (the word means "delight" or "pleasantness") and placed the man within it. As Bonhoeffer asks, "What will a man of the desert think of but a land with beautiful streams and trees full of fruit?"[1] Other riches are listed as well—gold, bdellium (probably a deep red mineral such as the ruby or garnet), and onyx. Despite the specific mention of lands (Havilah, Cush, Assyria) and rivers (Pishon, Gihon, Tigris [also known as the Hiddekel], Euphrates), there is now no common agreement among scholars regarding the location of Eden.* But if the site is uncertain, the meaning is clear: the Lord God provided lavishly for the man whom he had created. This is not to suggest that the man might while away his days in idleness, living effortlessly off the land. As in the first story he has the duty of exercising dominion over the created order, so here in the second account his responsibility is to "till it and keep it."

Special attention is called to the existence of two trees in the midst of the garden: the tree of life and the tree of the knowledge of good and evil. Both are signs, and both have a direct bearing on the life of the man. It is remarkable that there is no further reference to the first tree, the tree of life. It is simply there; and in being there fulfils its function. It is the sign of the life which the man already has from the God who created him. The fruit of this tree presents no temptation to the man because he already has life. The man does not eat of the fruit of the tree of life.

The tree of the knowledge of good and evil is the sign of what the man does *not* have and does not know. Living in innocence, and in unbroken obedience to God, the man has no experience of good or evil. The issue has not arisen. Nevertheless, it is present; the possibility of evil exists, and what is at stake is nothing less than the man's own life. "You may freely eat of every tree of the garden" (v. 16) corresponds to

---

*A dictionary of the Bible will acquaint the reader with the difficulties of assigning a location to Eden.

"Behold, I have given you every plant yielding seed which is upon the face of all the earth, and every tree with seed in its fruit; you shall have them for food" (1:29). This is the general (and generous) rule to which there is but one exception: "of the tree of the knowledge of good and evil you shall not eat." God knows what is involved in the issue of good and evil, and what the consequences of disobedience must be. He freely shares this knowledge with his creature, for God's command— his prohibition—is followed immediately by a warning: "for in the day that you eat of it you shall die."

It is important for us to recognize that although this warning constitutes a threat to the man's life, it is not God's threat. The threat to the man's survival is inherent in the knowledge of good and evil; and in sharing his knowledge of the inevitable outcome of eating the fruit of this tree God is simply alerting his creature to the danger. That God did inform the man is therefore an act of pure grace. By way of illustration: a mother takes her young child to the kitchen, and pointing to the flame coming from one of the burners on the stove tells the child, "This flame is very hot; if you touch it you will be burned." The threat to the child's safety does not come from the mother's words; it is inherent in the possibility that the child (having had no previous experience of being burned) may touch the flame. The mother's words of warning, like those of God to his creature, are prompted by her care and concern for one whom she loves very dearly.

The knowledge of good and evil is not a characteristic or an attribute of the man as created. This knowledge is rather the unique function and prerogative of God; and it radically and fundamentally distinguishes the Creator from the creature. It belongs to God alone to decide what is beyond man's province. It was God's decision to create the heavens and the earth, to bring order out of chaos, to rebuke the darkness and affirm the light. He willed that there be being rather than nonbeing—life rather than void. And it was also his will that the man not eat of the tree of the knowledge of good and evil. And on the completion of all his work he found it to be very good.

Is God's will now to be subject to a second opinion—that of the creature? Is the man now to encroach on the domain which is exclusively God's? Is the creature, born of dust, now to question the will of his Creator? Here we have the first intimation of the possibility of man's arrogance. The situation thus described calls to mind the word of God as proclaimed by the prophet Isaiah: "My glory I give to no other" (Isa. 42:8; 48:11). Human life is to be lived in open acknowledgement and joyful acceptance of God as Creator and Lord, and as such the sole judge of what is good and what is evil.

2:18 – 20 *Then the LORD God said, "It is not good that the man should be alone; I will make him a helper fit for him." . . .* Here again, as in 1:26, God takes counsel with himself in the matter of creating a human being. Of central importance to the creation of the woman is the account of the creation of the beasts of the field and the birds of the air, because if a proper helper was to be found for the man, it would have to be one in whom he would recognize his *alter ego*—his other self. He would have to be able to choose from among several possible helpers if he was to be said to have made a decision in this matter. The man was not to be placed in the position of having no alternatives. Accordingly, when God decided to make a helper for the man, he did not immediately begin making the woman. Rather, he formed the beasts and the birds, and he brought them to the man to see what he would call them. "Whatever the man called every living creature, that was its name." For the ancient Hebrew, to ascribe a name to a place, a person, or an object was to make a statement about it. As a rule, a name indicated a prominent characteristic or attribute of—or impression made by—a person or place or object (e.g., *Marah*: "bitterness"; *Sarah*: "princess"; *Yohanan* [John]: "God has been gracious"). So when God commissioned the man to give names to the beasts and the birds, he was asking the man what he thought of these creatures. However, it is very probable that the man did not feel enough involved with any of these creatures for one of them to qualify as a "helper." Nothing about them corresponded to what he knew himself to be. And in naming them, he indicated this. "He could not recognize them as his equals, and he could not choose them as his helpmeets" (Barth). They were simply not his kind. Accordingly, "for the man there was not found a helper fit for him."

36

2:21 – 25 *So the* LORD *God caused a deep sleep to fall upon the man. . . .* Our narrator moves on to the climax of his story—the completion of the creation of mankind. The significance of the divinely induced sleep is essentially that the man had no part in the creation of the woman—that is, in the completion of his own creation. For that is what we are being taught here: the completion of man (mankind) by the creation of woman. Up to this point the man is lone, and lonely; and God has pronounced that circumstance "not good" (v. 18)—which means, not in accordance with his will for man. The formation of the woman from the rib of the man signifies that she is "of" the man and "for" the man; not in the sense that she *belongs* to him, but rather that she belongs *with* him. As the text makes abundantly clear, she is brought before him as God's gift, not as his possession. And that relationship endures. For the man to regard or to treat the woman as though she had become his property is an obscene violation of the creation ordinance. The woman is a human being in her own right and has her own existence apart from that of the man, as one created by God. And in being presented to the man she does not cease to belong to God.

"This at last is bone of my bones."

The words "at last" refer back to the creation of the animals and birds, and their being brought before the man to see what he would call them. On that occasion it seems clear that the man was unenthusiastic, indifferent, and noncommittal to the prospect of any of these creatures as a helper. As companions (or, perhaps, enemies), yes; as helpers, no. But what a contrast when the woman is brought before him! Immediate and joyful recognition and enthusiastic welcome! The man receives, accepts, and acknowledges the woman as his counterpart, his helper, his *alter ego*. She is his own kind. With the creation of the woman, *adam* (humanity) has become whole. The "I-Thou" relationship is established; and in that respect (see 1:26) man is made in the image of God.

In celebration of the affinity which the man recognizes as existing between them, he calls her *Ishshah* ("Woman"), which is the feminine form of his own individuality as a man—*ish*. In verse 24 our narrator, with the historical reality of marriage in mind, adds the comment, "Therefore a man leaves his father

37

and his mother and cleaves to his wife, and they become one flesh." Although this observation is doubtless editorial in nature, it is not on that account to be ignored. We may properly judge its significance in that Jesus used this sentence as a word of the Creator when replying to the Pharisees on the question of divorce (Matt. 19:4). This insertion means that the coming together of man and woman in marriage is not merely a human convention but is a creation ordinance, and as such is valid before God.

Where there is no guilt and no disgrace, there is also no shame. The nakedness and absence of shame of "the man and his wife" are testimony to their innocence. So ends the second account of creation—an ending not unlike that of the first story, in which God saw what he had made and found it "very good."

CHAPTER SIX

A Parable of the Entry of Sin into Human Life

3:1 *Now the serpent was more subtle than any other wild creature that the* LORD *God had made.* In view of what is related in the following verses this opening statement seems hardly necessary. The serpent did not commence with a frontal attack on God's word and man's obedience to it, but with a question, addressed to the woman: "Did God say . . . ?" The inquiry is doubtless intended as a ploy, to seem to show deep concern for understanding correctly what God had said to the man and woman. Put another way, the serpent asks, What, precisely, did God say? And, Are you sure you heard him correctly? There is also an element of incredulity which the serpent wishes the woman to share. We may paraphrase it thus: "Is it conceivable that God really said. . . ? Surely there has been some mistake!" And finally, it is a religious question—a question about the word of God; the woman can scarcely take exception to an inquiry of this nature!

"Did God say, 'You shall not eat of any tree of the garden'?"

The serpent is careful to quote God incorrectly, such that its question cannot be answered by a simple yes or no—which would bring the conversation to an abrupt close. By the way in which the question is asked, the prohibition in God's earlier command to the man and woman is emphasized at the expense of the true nature of his word—namely, grace. The words of the serpent may be paraphrased as follows: "Has God placed you in the midst of these abundant riches and at the same time forbidden you to participate and share in any of them?"

It would be a great mistake if we were to regard the serpent's question as having been asked once and for all, "long ago and far away," and therefore as having no meaning and no relevance in contemporary society. On the contrary, the question for you and me is the same: "Did God say . . . ?" Or, "Has God said . . . ?" And it is being asked among us every day of every year of our lives in a variety of forms and contexts. It is true, of course, that the setting and the circumstances in which the question is asked is not exactly the same for any of us, but the question is identical. For example, Has God said, "You shall love your neighbor as yourself"? Is this really God's word to us today? But, we ask, are there not some exceptions in the light of which this exhortation need not be taken seriously—blacks, native North Americans, or perhaps Pakistanis? Has God said, "Thou shalt not kill"? It may be that we have misunderstood this commandment in the past. Surely there are circumstances in which it need not be strictly adhered to! What bearing, for example, does this prohibition have on waging war? On capital punishment? On euthanasia? And may it be said to apply equally to the unborn? Has God said, "Thou shalt not commit adultery"? Perhaps he did not mean it just the way it sounds; in which case, and in the light of the immense pressures of today's society, might not room be made for the practice of what is sometimes politely misnamed the "new morality"?

These are but a few of the areas in which the question which the woman faced (and later the man) faces us today.

3:2–3 *And the woman said to the serpent. . . .* The woman corrects the error in the serpent's question by repeating almost word for word what God has said, and adds: "neither shall you touch it"—thus enlarging on the severity of God's commandment. It may be that at this point the serpent is already making progress in its evil design, in persuading the woman to engage in conversation rather than to dismiss the matter out of hand. And it is also possible that the woman is beginning to see the word of God as restricting her freedom rather than protecting her best interests.

3:4 *But the serpent said to the woman, "You will not die."* For those who wish to take lessons in speaking the truth while also telling a lie, there is no more accomplished a tutor than the serpent. It told the truth: the man and woman did *not* die when they ate the fruit; but it lied: they became subject to death. To confirm and substantiate the truth of its lie the serpent pursues the matter further: "For God knows that when you eat of it your eyes will be opened, and you will be like God, knowing good and evil."

From Genesis 1:26 we have already learned that God made man in his image, after his likeness. The woman may have wondered, What possible harm can there be in wishing to be even more like God? What is involved in the confrontation of the woman by the serpent is whether mankind will be content with that likeness which God has given him as creature, or whether he will aspire to a likeness which is akin to divinity, and which consists in participation in the divine nature. Will he be satisfied, as creature, to live from God's grace, or will he prefer to live from his own resources—setting his own standards, choosing his own path, going his own way, and making his own decisions concerning right and wrong? The crux of the matter is whether man will let God be to him a gracious God.

The knowledge of good and evil—discerning, determining, controlling, and prescribing right and wrong, morality and immorality, salvation and perdition, life and death—is the unique attribute and the exclusive prerogative of divinity. Man acquires it only at his peril. To have this awesome knowledge and responsibility—to be like God in this sense—and not *be* God, is man's undoing. As a created being, man is not the source of his own life; neither is he able to prolong or perpetuate it. Alienated from the Creator who made him, cut off from the God who sustains him, and incapable of bearing the burden of the knowledge of good and evil, man can only die.

3:6 *So when the woman saw that the tree was good for food....* In the judgment of the woman, the tree was appealing on three counts: it could give nourishment, it was attractive to the eye, and it gave promise of wisdom far beyond the wisdom of obedience to the word of God, which she already possessed. There is an axiom that tells us it is not always wise to judge by appearances; but our narrator makes it plain that this is just what the woman did. (The same theme is taken up in 1 John 2:16.)

41

Accordingly, "she took of its fruit and ate; and she also gave some to her husband, and he ate."

We are not told the details of our first parents' transgression. This omission is evidently deliberate. We ask, Why is the story so indefinite, and its setting so seemingly innocuous? What could be so harmless as eating the fruit of a tree that was obviously "good for food"? Would it not have been an improvement to tell the story of man's fall into sin in more concrete terms—an account, for example, of theft, lying, brutality, or perhaps of sexual deviation? But the writer does not do this, and most likely for good reason. He tells the story in such a way that we understand man's defection not merely as a moral lapse but as rebellion, as revolt, as in fact man's rejection of God. We seem to see this more clearly if the incident—the eating of the good fruit—is, in itself, quite innocent. Seen in the light of God's prohibition, it is unmistakably an act of gross disobedience. The *occasion* of man's fall is his eating of the fruit of the tree of the knowledge of good and evil; the *cause* of his fall is his disobedience of the word of God.

3:7 *Then the eyes of both were opened.* In this moment, they saw themselves and each other as they had been, and they saw themselves and each other as they were now. They knew that they had been innocent, and that they were now guilty—guilty before God and in the presence of each other. They knew shame and embarrassment for the first time, as their recourse to fig leaves indicates.

The first—and devastating—effect of the knowledge of good and evil is an immediate perversion and deterioration of the relationship between the man and the woman. They now experience shame in something of which there is no need to be ashamed—their sexual differentiation.

3:8–13 *And they heard the sound of the LORD God walking in the garden in the cool of the day.* . . . God comes, man flees; God appears, man hides; God speaks, man answers. God does not come accusing man of sin and threatening punishment. He comes asking a question: "Where are you?" Man does not answer the question; rather he blurts out the whole miserable truth. "I was afraid, because I was naked; and I hid myself."

These words are confirmation that man now knows shame, and they are also the first intimation of the presence of conscience. While man lived in innocence and in perfect harmony with the word of God, the question of conscience could not arise. In that sense, conscience is a product of man's disobedience. It is evident that man has become "like God," knowing good and evil, setting his own standards and choosing his own course.

Many people regard conscience as "the voice of God" within them—a somewhat divine element in the human psyche or soul; but there is no biblical warrant for such an understanding. Rather, conscience is the voice of the man and woman who, as the serpent had promised, have become like God and are now making their own decisions concerning good and evil. Conscience is man's own voice in his new-found capacity as judge of good and evil. It is a device by means of which man can be at peace within himself even when he is no longer in fellowship with God. Bonhoeffer states: "Conscience is not the voice of God to sinful man; it is man's defence against it." By way of example, he writes, "Conscience says, 'Adam, you are naked, hide yourself from the Creator, you dare not stand before him.' God says, 'Adam, stand before me.' "[1] Bonhoeffer also comments on the folly and irony of this situation—it is *because* he is a sinner that man *should* stand before God!

In addition to being the voice of man, conscience has a second function as well. Because of its origin in man's disobedience it is a constant (and unwelcome?) reminder of his fall, and that there *is* a word of God which is to be heard and heeded.

The man does stand before God, but his words are evasive and accusatory. He blames his sinful act on "the woman whom thou gavest to be with me." The man's defence of his action is, This would never have happened if you had not given me the woman. You and the woman must share the responsibility for what has happened.

God now turns to the woman: "What is this that you have done?" The woman is similarly evasive: "The serpent beguiled me, and I ate." The woman does not accuse, except, perhaps, by implication: it was you, God, who created the serpent. Neither the man nor the woman has surrendered, neither has repented, and neither recognizes this conversation for what it truly is: God's patience and grace.

3:14 – 15 *The* LORD *God said to the serpent.* . . . In the narrative of the Fall the serpent has played the part of the voice of temptation—the subverter of mankind—and has brought to ruin the fairest and noblest of all God's creation. Yet for all its vaunted sublety the serpent is not able to escape the wrath of the Creator. It will continue to move on its belly, but now grovelling, despised, and hated—its posture a constant reminder of its infamy. Its diet will necessarily include the dust on which it crawls. It is interesting that many centuries later the disciples were instructed to shake the dust off their feet as a testimony against those who refused to hear the gospel (Matt. 10:14). And there is more to the curse on the serpent.

"I will put enmity between you and the woman, and between your seed and her seed."

There will be constant and unremitting antagonism between the serpent (that is, the voice of temptation, the power of evil, by whatever names it may subsequently be known: devil, demon, dragon, satan, anti-Christ) for untold generations to come. It will be an unequal contest, which the serpent cannot hope to win, for the Lord is and will remain on the side of mankind. "He [the seed of the woman] shall bruise your [the seed of the serpent] head, and you [the serpent] shall bruise his [the seed of the woman] heel." This verse suggests the age-long struggle that mankind will always have to wage against the power of sin, culminating in victory by and for the seed of the woman (humanity). The bruising of the head suggests that the serpent's wound will be fatal; the bruising of the heel is a warning that even the victor will not come away unscathed.

The early Christian commentators called these words "Protevangelium," that is, "the first proclamation of the gospel" or "the first announcement of a Savior." Certainly they are prophetic words, but the narrator is probably seeking to express his profound confidence that God would see to the restoration of all things. From our modern-day perspective we can see that Jesus, born of Mary, was indeed of the seed of woman, that he resisted temptation, paid the penalty of sin (not his own), and was victorious over death. He did not do this at no cost; he did not come away unscathed. But sin no longer has the power to condemn to death those who believe in him.

3:16 *I will greatly multiply your pain in child-bearing. . . .* The joyful promise of giving life—of bearing children—is now mingled with pain (RSV) and sorrow (KJV); hence the phrase "the sorrows of Eve." We also learn that the woman's desire is for her husband, "and he shall rule over you." This is the first reference to the primacy of the man. There could have been no question of primacy while the man and woman lived together in complete harmony and obedience to the word of God. Rule is necessary only where disorder has set in—in this case as a consequence of their disobedience. Thus, this new order in which the woman is subject to the man is, like the emergence of conscience, a product of their fall from grace. It is important for us to observe that this decision by God, this appointment to authority, has nothing whatever to do with the question of a superiority, real or imagined, of one partner over the other. That question does not arise out of this situation. That is to say, by making him "ruler" God does not make the man superior. The question of superiority is *ultra vires*: out of order. The appointment of the man to rule is God's gracious provision in the face of possible discord between the man and woman.

3:17 – 19 *Cursed is the ground because of you. . . .* God's punishment of the man does not first of all fall upon his person, but upon the ground. We have learned (2:15) that work is not a curse, but because of sin an element of drudgery enters into man's work. Wilhelm Vischer makes the following comment on this verse: "Instead of enjoying the fruits of paradise as the gardener with the care-free spirit of a child, he must work laboriously to win food from the earth."[2] His own life will depend upon his labor—now in an uncongenial environment which also brings forth "thorns and thistles." Accordingly, it is only by the "sweat of [his] face" that the man shall eat bread. Yet for all man's striving to stay alive, he is not equal to the task. In due time—God's time—he will return to the place of his origin. He does not have the quality of life within himself; he is mortal, and must return to the dust.

3:20 *The man called his wife's name Eve, because she was the mother of all living.* This may well be at once the most astounding, the most profound, and the most exuberant thing the man ever did. We might reconstruct the situation as follows: having heard his own death sentence pronounced, the man remembers something the Lord had said earlier, and he stakes his hopes on it. He recalls the Lord God talking about the seed of the woman, and now recognizes its significance. Even in a world destined to die, there is, by God's grace, the hope—nay, the promise—of life. In joyful acknowledgement and celebration of God's *merciful* anger, the man gives his wife the name "Eve" (derived from the Hebrew verb "to be"; hence: "the mother of all who become"). Even those destined to die may pass on the precious gift of life. Death, implacable as it is, does not have the last word!

3:21 *And the LORD God made for Adam and for his wife garments of skins, and clothed them.* Vischer states: "No cult of nudism . . . can restore the innocence of paradise."[3] Nudism denies man's shame, and in doing so denies the reality of the Fall. God affirms man's guilt, and makes provision for it. He confirms the propriety of man's instinctive action (sewing fig leaves) and provides a more substantial remedy (garments of skins). But even this is not permanent, and it is not a cure. It is like a band-aid—pending the more comprehensive treatment when we will be clothed in the righteousness of God's own Son, Jesus Christ. "For in this we groan, earnestly desiring to be clothed upon with our house which is from heaven: if so be that being clothed we shall not be found naked. For we that are in this tabernacle do groan, being burdened: not for that we would be unclothed, but clothed upon, that mortality might be swallowed up of life" (2 Cor. 5:2–4, KJV).

Two hymns of the church proclaim this hope.

> When He shall come with trumpet sound,
>   Oh, may I ever then be found
> Clothed in His righteousness alone
>   Faultless to stand before the throne!
>   —*Edward Mote*

Jesus, Thy blood and righteousness
My beauty are, my glorious dress;
'Midst flaming worlds, in these arrayed,
With joy shall I lift up my head.
—*Nicholas L. von Zinzendorf*

3:22–24 *Then the* LORD *God said, "Behold, the man has become like one of us, knowing good and evil. . . ."* The serpent's words (3:5)—"You will be like God"—are now confirmed by God. Man *has* become like God; he knows good and evil. And on the basis of this knowledge he presumes to govern his own life. He is now his own god, and must live from his own resources. But, having been told that "to dust you shall return," he knows that to live is impossible. He does not have life within himself; he is mortal, and holds his tenure of life only at God's good pleasure. Bonhoeffer comments: "The will to live, the inability to live, having to live—that is the living death of the man who is like God."[4] It is to this situation and torment that Paul referred when he cried out: "Wretched man that I am! Who will deliver me from this body of death?" (Rom. 7:24). But he had seen the answer to his dilemma and was grateful: "Thanks be to God through Jesus Christ our Lord!" (v. 25).

But Adam does not know about Jesus Christ. It is possible that in seeking relief from his distress he might seek out the tree of life. And so God speaks: "Now, lest he put forth his hand and take also of the tree of life, and eat, and live for ever—" (v. 22). God seems to stop speaking in mid-sentence, and we then read: "Therefore the LORD God sent him forth from the garden of Eden, to till the ground from which he was taken. He drove out the man . . ." (vv. 23–24).

There is an unmistakable element of compulsion in these words. The man did not wish to leave the garden, and he did not do so of his own accord. He was "sent"—"driven." The tree of life is now inaccessible, and man's yearning for life on his own terms is denied. Now he lives only on the way to death. As we read in Thomas Gray, "The paths of glory lead but to the grave."[5]

At the close of this most tragic chapter of the Bible we read:

"and at the east of the garden of Eden he placed the cherubim."* With the precautions that God has taken there is no possibility of man returning to Eden; and so the tree of life is unapproachable. This is the first of many references to cherubim in the Bible, and their most frequent function is that of guardians. They symbolize the presence of God, so that it is God himself who stands guard against man's return. The expulsion is complete, and irreversible during man's lifetime. Man must live, and contend, and die—and only then "to him who conquers I will grant to eat of the tree of life, which is in the paradise of God" (Rev. 2:7).

*(Cherub; plural: cherubim). "The facts at present available indicate an order of angels" (*Westminster Dictionary of the Bible*).

Chapter Seven

A Parable of the Spread of Sin in Human Society

4:1 *Now Adam knew Eve his wife, and she conceived and bore Cain, saying, "I have gotten a man with the help of the* Lord*."* In the Hebrew language the meaning of the word here translated "knew" is not limited to knowledge of an academic or intellectual nature. It signifies something much deeper and more profound. To know in this sense is to experience, or to have experience of, something or someone. Christians, for example, frequently make a similar distinction between knowing *about* God (that is, having heard or read about him) and *knowing* God (that is, having experienced his presence and power). The word *knew* refers here to sexual union.

Eve's comment on the birth of Cain was that she had "gotten a man with the help of the Lord." Today we often think of human birth as perfectly natural, as if no divine intervention or oversight were required. Eve, however, was closer to the truth that Scripture proclaims: "Lo, sons are a heritage from the Lord, the fruit of the womb a reward" (Ps. 127:3; see also Ps. 128).

4:2 *And again, she bore his brother Abel.* A man, his wife, and two sons. Human society is formed—in miniature, certainly—but human society nevertheless. Each goes about his business: Abel as a shepherd, Cain as a farmer.

4:3 – 5a *Cain brought to the* Lord *an offering of the fruit of the ground, and Abel brought of the firstlings of his flock and of* *their fat portions. And the LORD had regard for Abel and his offering, but for Cain and his offering he had no regard.* There is no evidence in Scripture that God prefers the sacrifice of animals to that of grain and fruit. And there is no indication in the text that he held one brother to be more worthy than the other. What, then, are we to make of his acceptance of the one and his rejection of the other? On the face of it, it appears to be an arbitrary decision—even discriminatory, and therefore offensive. If we are to understand this passage of Scripture, we must assemble all the elements of the story, and give to each its proper bearing and emphasis.

We begin with the God who called man into being as an act of pure love and out of a desire to have an "other" who would be his partner and counterpart. And he made the man in his own image and likeness. The man knowingly fell victim to temptation and through his willful disobedience became estranged from God. In punishment he was expelled from the garden, and the warm, intimate relationship between the Creator and the creature was strained to the breaking point. The announced penalty for man's disobedience was death; but the man did not die; in his great mercy God spared him.

Cain and Abel are now born to Adam and Eve. They are the children of fallen parents in a fallen world. As such they are both aware that they stand before God as their parents do: alienated from him and in need of forgiveness and reconciliation. We may be confident of this because the brothers come before God with sacrifices, in open acknowledgement of their need of atonement. As we have seen, what Cain and Abel bring as a sacrifice is not the reason God does not accept Cain's sacrifice. Indeed, all the fruit of the field and every creature already belong to God. Thus, whatever God may do in this instance will be a matter of sheer grace on his part.

How can this essential element of grace in this story (and indeed in the gospel) be most clearly portrayed and demonstrated in this situation? How can the teaching of God's free and undeserved grace to man be presented so as to ensure that it is not misconstrued by successive generations of his people? For this is what is at stake in the story of Cain and Abel.

There are now three possibilities in this narrative. First, God may see fit to reject both offerings. Neither of the men has any legitimate claim on him, and he is under no obligation to pardon either of them. He certainly does not *need* their gifts. What would be more natural than that he should ignore both men and both sacrifices? If God were to do that, however, he would not be showing himself to be the merciful God that he is. He would be revealing himself as unforgiving, unloving, uncaring, and (haughtily) indifferent to man's plight. And that is not what God is, and it is not how he wishes to be known.

A second possibility is that God may see fit to accept both men and both offerings. (This is what most people, on a first reading of the story, undoubtedly want to be told.) Yet this, too, would lend itself to misunderstanding. If God were to have accepted both sacrifices, we would be encouraged to believe that man could *earn* God's pardon—in this case by the work of his hands. Forgiveness would then become a saleable commodity, with God as the Vendor. It would be an exchange, a transaction, as the prophet Micah observed (and discounted), "Shall I give my first-born for my transgression, the fruit of my body for the sin of my soul?" (Mic. 6:7). On this (mis)understanding it is even conceivable that God's displeasure might be assuaged by man's tributes to him. We would hesitate to use the word *bribery* in this connection except that it is used by Jehoshaphat when, in appointing judges in the cities of Judah, he warned that "there is no perversion of justice with the LORD our God, or partiality, or taking bribes" (2 Chron. 19:7). We content ourselves then in saying simply that the God who reveals himself in the Bible is not open to this kind of approach.

The third possibility, and the one which in fact God adopts, is to accept one offering and to disregard the other. In this way we are being told that God is not uncaring and unloving and that he is not indifferent to the fate of his errant creature. He has not abandoned the world and does not forsake his people. He accepts Abel and his offering not because he needs it, or even wants it, but purely because of grace. He rejects Cain's offering lest his grace should be obscured and we should be misled into believing that one or both of the brothers earned or merited pardon by virtue of the intrinsic value of their sacrifices.

(Acceptance and rejection is a recurring theme throughout

the Bible, Old Testament and New. It begins with Cain and
Abel, and as we shall see shortly is picked up again with Cain
and his descendants and Seth and his children up to Noah.)

Turning from the Old Testament to the New we find that
Paul's view of God's acceptance and rejection as sheer grace
confirms what has been said above. With reference to the births
of Jacob and Esau, Rebecca was told that Esau, the oldest
son, would serve Jacob, the younger brother, "in order that
God's purpose of election* might continue, not because of
works but because of his [God's] call" (Rom. 9:11). "So it
[election] depends not upon man's will or exertion, but upon
God's mercy" (Rom. 9:16).

There is a further question to be asked concerning the story
of Cain and Abel's sacrifices, namely, Why is the story told in
such a way that it is Abel's sacrifice that proves acceptable to
God rather than Cain's? Is there anything for us to learn from
the acceptance of an animal sacrifice? Many biblical scholars
see in this narrative the first clear indication that the sin that
alienates man from God requires nothing less than the forfeit-
ing of life itself if reconciliation is to be achieved. If this is the
case, the story of Cain and Abel may be seen as a forerunner
of the elaborate framework of sacrifices which lies at the heart
of Old Testament religion as practised in Israel, for as we learn
from the Letter to the Hebrews, "under the law almost everything is purified with blood, and without the shedding of blood
there is no forgiveness of sins" (9:22). In the New Testament,
with its witness to the life, death, and resurrection of Christ,
the *practice* of offering sacrifices ceased, but the *principle* remains. In these latter days it is Jesus Christ, "the Lamb of
God," who by giving his life a ransom for many has taken
away the sin of the world (Matt. 20:28; John 1:29). And "when
Christ had offered for all time a single sacrifice for sins, he sat
down at the right hand of God" (Heb. 10:12). It is this single
sacrifice that we commemorate in the Eucharist and the Lord's
Supper, for "this cup is the new covenant in my blood. . . .

*"elect": this word is used only four times in the Old Testament (KJV), all in
Isaiah, and means "those whom God has chosen" or accepted. Its use is fairly
common in the New Testament in both the Gospels and the Letters, where it
refers to Jewish and Gentile Christians, i.e., the church.

As often as you eat this bread and drink the cup, you proclaim the Lord's death until he comes'' (1 Cor. 11:25–26).

4:5b – 7 *Cain was very angry, and his countenance fell. . . .* The Lord speaks lovingly to Cain. He asks, "Why are you angry, and why has your countenance fallen?" God stands ready to receive even those whom he has once rejected. The door is always open and a ready welcome awaits us. The Lord also has a warning for Cain: "If you do not do well, sin is couching at the door [ready to pounce]." Sin *wants* Cain—wants to possess him as its servant. But God warns, "You must master it."

4:8 – 9 *Cain said to Abel his brother, "Let us go out to the field. . . ."* Cain does not master sin; sin masters Cain. God's warning goes unheeded and he and Abel go to the field. Cain is unwilling to kill his brother in the presence of their parents, but he does not hesitate to kill him in the presence of God. "Then the LORD said to Cain, 'Where is Abel your brother?' " Unlike his father Adam, Cain does not take refuge in flight, he takes refuge in a lie: "I do not know; am I my brother's keeper?" This piece of incredible impertinence has become a celebrated phrase in the English language. Am I responsible for my brother's well-being? Throughout the whole Bible we are taught that the answer to this question is an unqualified yes. We are commanded to give help to those who need it and to provide as generously as we are able for the care of others. We do this because God has laid this responsibility on us all.

4:10 – 16 *"What have you done? The voice of your brother's blood is crying to me from the ground. And now you are cursed from the ground. . . ."* Cain is unable to conceal his guilt; God is angry and lays a curse on him. He has been a farmer, but now the ground will no longer yield its fruit for his labors. "You shall be a fugitive and a wanderer on the earth." Cain now turns from God in shame and despair and cries, "My punishment is greater than I can bear."* However this may be

*Luther translates: "My sin is greater than can be forgiven." Quoted with approval by both Barth and Vischer.

translated, it is clear that Cain has lost the arrogance he once displayed. He is now without hope. He has been driven from the ground, and banished from God's presence. He will be in constant flight and in perpetual fear for his life. Cain has been brought to his knees—but God comes to him and lifts him up! "Not so!" God responds. God himself will be Cain's protector, and he assures him that his life will be spared. The mark that God places on Cain is the mark of a murderer; but it is also the sign of his mercy and boundless love!

"Then Cain went away from the presence of the LORD, and dwelt in the land of Nod, east of Eden." Nod probably means "wandering"; and, like Eden, its location is unknown.

In the story of Cain and Abel we have, in miniature, a portrayal of mankind at its violent worst. Genesis 3 shows us man's relationship with God radically changed by sin. Our present narrative confirms this, illustrating the dire consequences of sin for human relationships as well. In the person of Cain we have seen jealousy (of his brother), rage and hatred (against both God and Abel), capital crime (murder), and falsehood (to God). "Sin came into the world through one man and death through sin, and so death spread to all men because all men sinned" (Rom. 5:12). It is as though sin were a virus which, having gained a foothold in our "first parents," spreads into human society, contaminating all its members. Man's sin is a personal but not a private matter; it affects others as well.

4:17–24 *Cain knew his wife, and she conceived and bore Enoch; and he built a city and called the name of the city after the name of his son, Enoch. . . .* These verses list the family of Cain. Our narrator takes it for granted that the earth is sufficiently populated so that a city can be formed. The old chestnut, Where did Cain's wife come from? is ignored as if to say it has no relevance to the main theme of the chapter. The descendants of Cain are listed: some are nomads who deal in livestock; some are musicians; and some fashion tools of bronze and iron.

In this way our narrator tells of the beginnings of what we call civilization and commerce. It is what is known in the New Testament as "the world." It is secular culture. The biblical attitude towards civilization is always twofold. Richardson states in his commentary on Genesis 1–11: "All the gifts and blessings of civilization are from God; yet the advance of civilization does not of itself make men more reverent towards God or more humane towards one another. [See Lamech's boasts and pride in having killed a man for merely striking him—Gen. 4:23–24.] Every new invention or art of civilization, from the discovery of copper and iron to that of nuclear fission, can and has been turned to man's destruction and hurt. . . . It [the secular world] is under the mark of Cain . . . yet preserved from annihilation by the grace of God."[1]

4:25–26 *And Adam knew his wife again, and she bore a son and called his name Seth. . . . At that time men began to call upon the name of the LORD.* A new line of descent from Adam and Eve is begun with the birth of Seth. It is traced more fully in the next chapter, but immediately Eve recognizes that the birth of her third son is by God's "appointment" to take the place of Abel. Accordingly she names him Seth, which means "set" or "appointed" or "established"—a firm foundation.

The mention of men calling on the name of the Lord marks Seth, his son Enosh, and their descendants as a worshiping community, as distinguished from the children of Cain. It is for this reason that the early church theologians regarded these verses and the following chapter as indicative of the emerging church; that is, the people of God. The *form* of the church as we know it was not present, and the word *church* does not appear anywhere in the Old Testament, but the *reality*—people worshiping God, calling on his name, trusting in his mercy— is very much in evidence.

5:1–32 *This is the book of the generations of Adam. . . .* The entire fifth chapter of Genesis is given over to tracing the lineage of Adam through Seth and Enosh. The language and structure of verses 1b–2 are so remarkably similar to that of 1:26a and 27 that we are probably correct in assuming that both come from the same source.

There are several items of particular interest and importance in this genealogy. First, our narrator is undoubtedly concerned to set the stage for the story which is to follow—the flood.

He does so by establishing the ancestry of Noah, the chosen of God, and in a most direct manner: Adam, Seth, Enosh, Kenan, Mahalalel, Jared, Enoch, Methuselah, Lamech, and Noah—ten in all. It is evident that this is a selective list of names.

It is possible that in this genealogical table, as in others of ancient times, links in the chain have been omitted and only the more prominent names are mentioned. An example of this practice may be found in Matthew 1, where the names of three kings of Judah (Ahaziah, Joash, and Amaziah) are omitted and Joram is said to have begotten Uzziah, who was in fact his great-great-grandson (Matt. 1:8).

A second item of interest in this genealogy is that, of the ten patriarchs named here, only two are accorded comment in addition to birth, name, and lifespan. The first is Enoch, of whom it is said that he "walked with God; and he was not, for God took him" (v. 24). This is the first of only four such instances recorded in Scripture—Enoch, Moses, Elijah, and Jesus. Barth comments: "It was not death which removed him [Enoch] from this life, but God. . . . Enoch is seen and described as an instance in which there is no doubt whatever of the salvation which awaits man on the other side of the frontier of his time."[2]

Additional comment is also made in connection with the birth of Noah. Lamech called his son's name Noah, and said, "Out of the ground which the LORD has cursed this one shall bring us relief from our work and from the toil of our hands" (v. 29). The significance of Lamech's action in this verse is not easy to assess. Certainly we can say that he believed his son would play a decisive role in God's plan for the future of mankind, but this conviction is expressed in what for us today seem to be vague terms. It is evident, however, that Lamech has not lost hope in God, and recognizes that God has not abandoned his people. Perhaps the most we can say is that in the birth of Noah, Lamech is portrayed as one who sees, however indistinctly, "light at the end of the tunnel."

Finally, a brief comment on a question that is frequently asked concerning this genealogy. How are we to reconcile the ages ascribed to these patriarchs—from 365 years (Enoch) to 969 years (Methuselah)—with the "three score and ten" (Ps.

90:10) which has been the normal span of life for most of recorded history? In our quest for an answer to this problem we find no consensus among scholars, though several thoughtful suggestions have been put forward. At first glance the tabulation of ages and years seems to be totally irrelevant to the story; and this probably accounts for the opinion of one commentator that the figures are "entirely fanciful." Yet because of the precision which our author exercises in giving this information, this verdict does not seem convincing. A second explanation accepts the figures as valid, commenting on the immense vitality of mankind immediately after creation as compared with our own, and quoting Proverbs 10:27—"The fear of the Lord prolongs life, but the years of the wicked will be short." In this view, comparing the average life span of today with the ages in Genesis 5 shows that man's longevity has been eroded and undermined down through the years by sin.

CHAPTER EIGHT

A Parable of God's Attitude to Man's Sin

6:1–4 *When men began to multiply on the face of the ground. . . .* These verses are among the most difficult to understand in the whole of the Old Testament. One reason for this is their fragmentary nature. It is widely believed that they originally formed part of a longer document which, if it had been preserved, would have provided us with more explicit information. A second reason is that it appears to have more in common with pagan mythology than with the biblical message. The idea of there having been sexual union between the gods and human beings is not foreign to classical mythology; and many ancient peoples believed that supermen were the product of such unions. But if this is the case, what is the purpose of including a story such as this in Holy Writ? It can only be because it contains an important and even essential element of biblical truth.*

In our studies of the third and fourth chapters of Genesis we encountered, in turn, temptation, disobedience, evasiveness, fear, shame, guilt, pride, jealousy, deceit, anger, and murder. It has not been a pretty picture. The realization that all of these unsavory elements are part of our own daily life and experience strongly suggests that man's plight is more

---

*There are doubtless those who will find this idea of a commingling of pagan mythology with the Word of God distasteful and even unacceptable, and who will seek some alternate explanation. We recall in this connection, however, that the apostle Paul did something not unlike this in preaching to the Athenians gathered on Mars' Hill (Acts 17:16–34). He quotes from their own pagan poets to strengthen his point (v. 28). "In him we live and move and have our being" is from the writings of Epimenides the Cretan (596 B.C.). "For we are indeed his offspring" is from the *Phaenomena* of Aratus (310 B.C.).

grievous than mere aberration would account for. The sin of the world is much more than the sum total of the moral lapses of mankind. John writes that "the whole world is in the power of the evil one" (1 John 5:19), and Paul speaks of Jesus as the One "who gave himself for our sins to deliver us from the present evil age" (Gal. 1:4).

It is clear that verses 1–4 are intended to prepare us for verses 5–7, in which God sees nothing in his creation worth preserving and is determined to "blot out" man and beasts and creeping things and birds of the air. We are here being told something of the magnitude and pervasiveness of evil. The story of the disobedience of Adam and Eve in Genesis 3 is now supplemented and reinforced by a story of the illicit marriage of semidivine beings with the daughters of men. The consequences of the Fall are here portrayed as not only individual, personal, and societal, but *cosmic* in their nature and extent. It is the *world* that lies under the power of the evil one; it is the *age* that is evil. Evil permeates and pollutes the whole of reality apart from God. And this has come about by what is here depicted as an ungodly alliance of good and evil—giving rise to that which is truly demonic.* In the words of William Neil: "Evil has become endemic, a monstrous, supernatural, all-pervasive pollution. The atmosphere is saturated with it. . . . There is poison in the heart of it which suffuses and taints every aspect of life so that nothing that man can do is pure and holy."[1]

The apostle Paul finds this contradiction within his own person and confesses it in his Letter to the Romans: "I do not understand my own actions. For I do not do what I want, but I do the very thing I hate" (Rom. 7:15). And he tells the Ephesians that if in striving to be obedient we had only the lusts of the flesh to contend with we might have an even chance of success. But such is not the case, "for we are not contending against flesh and blood, but against the principalities, against

---

*The Crusades, or Holy Wars, of the tenth to mid-thirteenth centuries and the Inquisitions (especially in the Church of Rome during the Middle Ages and in response to the Protestant Reformation) may be cited as examples of the horrendous effects of the demonic liaison of good and evil. Both had their origin in religious zeal, and both resulted in the torture and death of millions of innocent people.

the powers, against the world rulers of this present darkness, against the spiritual hosts of wickedness in the heavenly places" (Eph. 6:12).

In this way the mythology of the Old Testament points to the truth of the New, and to the reality of the present day. For we, too, have our "Nephilim" (monsters) and our mighty men— the Bonapartes, Hitlers, Stalins, and Perons—whose paths are strewn with the mangled bodies of the innocent dead.

6:5–7 *The LORD saw that the wickedness of man was great in the earth, and that every imagination of the thoughts of his heart was only evil continually. And the LORD was sorry. . . .* It would be difficult to imagine a more complete and sweeping condemnation of the ways of man on the earth than is contained in these words. Twice we read that God was sorry he had made man; "it grieved him to his heart." He could not find a single redeeming feature in what man had made of creation. Under the circumstances, there appeared to be nothing to do but to destroy man.

It is well for us to observe that this situation has not changed materially to the present day. We still greet God's grace with our unfaithfulness, and his faithfulness with our disobedience. We continue to be the foolish virgins, the rich young rulers, and the unprofitable servants portrayed in the New Testament. "The LORD looks down from heaven upon the children of men, to see if there are any that act wisely, that seek after God. They have all gone astray, they are all alike corrupt; there is none that does good, no, not one" (Ps. 14:2,3). And Jesus' observation is also very much to the point: "No one is good but God alone" (Mark 10:18 and others).

6:11–13 *Now the earth was corrupt in God's sight, and the earth was filled with violence. And God saw the earth, and behold it was corrupt; for all flesh had corrupted their way upon the earth. And God said to Noah, "I have determined to make an end of all flesh. . . ."* In describing the cauldron of iniquity that the earth has become, our narrator uses repetition for effect. The depth of God's grief and sorrow is unspeakable. He will blot out man, beast, bird, and creeping thing, and "destroy the earth"—more in sorrow than in anger.

But wait!

6:8–10 *But Noah found favor [grace] in the eyes of the* LORD.
*. . . Noah was a righteous man, blameless in his generation;
Noah walked with God. . . .*In view of the thoroughgoing condemnation of humankind in verses 5–7 we may well ask the
nature of the righteousness and blamelessness of Noah, a mem-
ber of the same generation. The answer lies with God, not with
Noah. Noah's righteousness consists not in his personal rec-
titude, but solely in the Lord's acceptance of him. It is, again,
sheer grace. It belongs with the words of the psalmist, "Blessed
is the man to whom the LORD imputes no iniquity" (Ps. 32:2),
and with the statement that Abraham "believed the LORD; and
he reckoned it to him as righteousness" (Gen. 15:6). This theme,
the undeserved grace of God to man, is repeated again and
again in the Old Testament, and echoed and re-echoed in the
New. It takes up almost the whole of Romans 4; and the Old
Testament content of grace is spoken of in 2 Corinthians 5:19;
Hebrews 11:7; and James 2:23. It also appears in countless
other passages in which no reference is made to Old Testament
events and characters.

Thus Noah is accepted—chosen—for the sake of the human
race, in order that through *one man* mankind shall be preserved.

6:14–21 *Make yourself an ark of gopher wood. . . .* Noah, now
the friend and confidant of the Lord, receives the instructions
necessary for his survival. He is to make an ark—not a ship,
but a floating platform (covered, of course)—of gopher wood.
The word in Hebrew may indicate pine or cypress. It is to be
seaworthy and water-resistant, covered inside and out with
pitch. The dimensions are given: in our unit of measure this
would translate to approximately 450 feet long, 75 feet wide,
and 45 feet high. There were to be three decks, and the ark
was to be oblong in shape.

It is probably safe to say that many people today are ex-
tremely skeptical of reading the account of the flood in Genesis
as historical fact, preferring to regard the story as a quaint bit
of ancient folklore. Yet it is doubtful the matter can be dis-
missed quite so easily. The existence of other ancient stories
of a deluge is well known, the principal one being of Babylo-

nian origin. It is the opinion of Alan Richardson that the account of the flood entered Palestine from a Babylonian source.[2] And Neil reports: "Evidence was found at Ur in 1929 by Sir Leonard Woolley that a flood of some magnitude had covered that part of Mesopotamia in early times, possibly about 4000 B.C." He further suggests that "Basically, the Genesis story is taken from the common fund of Near Eastern tradition and is used by the biblical writers in characteristic fashion to teach a religious lesson."[3] In short, the occurrence of a deluge was common knowledge, or a shared memory, among many Near Eastern peoples of ancient times.

We have observed that in chapters 1 and 2 of Genesis there are two distinct stories of creation, and we believe that they come from two sources or traditions. Each of them tells its story in its own way, and they complement one another. A similar distinction can be made in the story of the flood, for many scholars detect two traditions woven together in the Noah narrative. Compare, for example, 6:19—"And of every living thing of all flesh, you shall bring two of every sort into the ark, to keep them alive with you; they shall be male and female," with 7:2—"Take with you seven pairs of all clean animals, the male and his mate; and a pair of the animals that are not clean, the male and his mate."* Consider also the duration of the flood. From 7:11 we learn that the flood began on the seventeenth day of the second month of Noah's six hundredth year, from 7:24 that the waters "prevailed" for one hundred and fifty days, and from 8:14 that "the earth was dry" after a little more than a year. But reading 7:12 and 8:6–12 together, we learn that the flood lasted forty days and forty nights, and that after what seems to be a period of perhaps only a few weeks, the earth was dry.

These two examples may suggest that what we have here are two stories from different sources joined together, with no attempt being made to reconcile the details. In any case, why do we find a story of a *flood* in literature that the church be-

---

*"Clean": fit for food or sacrifice; "unclean": unfit for food or sacrifice. Many people made such distinctions in ancient times. More specifically, *clean* referred to animals that parted the hoof *and* chewed the cud; *unclean* to animals not characterized by one or both of the above. Among aquatic creatures, only fish with fins and scales were edible. All birds were edible, except birds of prey such as vultures, eagles, ravens, and owls (because they eat blood and carrion). See a dictionary of the Bible for greater detail.

lieves to be the Word of God? One might reasonably suppose that an account of a prehistoric deluge would be of infinitely greater interest to archaeologists and paleontologists than to most people in the church. The reason is, of course, that this is primarily a story about God and man and the relationship between them; the narrative is simply the vehicle by which this relationship is portrayed.

The relationship between the Holy God and fallen man can be adequately expressed only by some such impossible paradox as we have before us: God's implacable determination to "make an end of all flesh" and the incomprehensible grace by which he preserves humanity. This, in a word, is the way of God's infinite patience with the sinner. We have seen it before and we will see it again, but never—until the time of Christ—with greater clarity, and not on the same scale. Under threat of death Adam disobeyed God, yet he was spared. Cain murdered his own brother and though expelled from the presence of God he was protected. But God is not One to accept defeat, whether by a disobedient Adam, a murderous Cain, a corrupt generation, an unfaithful Israel, or an apostate church. Barth comments: "The point of this story is that while God destroys the human race and all things living for the sake of His holiness and righteousness, He is at the same time concerned about the further progress and growth of the human race and of all other creatures."[4]

6:22; 7:1–10 *Noah did this; he did all that God commanded him....* We read in both 6:22 and 7:5 that Noah, following instructions meticulously, was obedient to the God who had placed him in mortal jeopardy, and who concurrently ensured his safety. Thus in 1 Peter 3:20 the ark drifting securely on the face of the threatening waters is seen as a type of the church, in which the people of God find refuge from the turbulence round about them. And Paul understands immersion in the waters of baptism as "burial" with Christ in his death, to the end that in being raised with him we "might walk in newness of life" (Rom. 6:4).

7:11–16 *On that day all the fountains of the great deep burst forth, and the windows of the heavens were opened. And rain* *fell upon the earth forty days and forty nights.* . . . Water came up from below, and it came down from above, in torrents. The family of eight—Noah and his wife, their three sons, and the three daughters-in-law—entered the ark, accompanied by an entourage of animals. "And the LORD shut him in."

Everything went according to plan (God's plan) for the duration of the flood, whether the forty days and forty nights or the one hundred and fifty days is preferred. It should be said at this point, however, that Scripture makes considerable use of the forty days and forty nights formula: Nineveh was given forty days to repent (Jonah 3:4); Jesus fasted for forty days in the wilderness prior to the temptations (Matt. 4:2); and his resurrection appearances took place over a span of forty days prior to his ascension (Acts 1:3). In each situation there is an element of danger until deliverance is assured. Therefore, the forty days is probably a typical formula rather than a literal period of time.

A striking feature of these stories, and indeed of the Bible in general, is the emphasis placed on God's genuine affection for his creatures other than mankind. We make no mistake in observing that there are some similarities in the way God deals with men and (in particular) the animal kingdom: both were created of the ground (2:7,19); both perish (Ps. 49:20); and both will share in the peace of the coming messianic age (Isa. 11:6–9; 65:25). Furthermore, we learn much concerning animals from the account of the flood: they suffer as a result of man's sin (6:7; 7:21–23); the preparation for the flood includes provision for their safety (6:19; 7:2–3, 8–9, 14–16); they are "remembered" by God (8:1); and the covenant with Noah and his descendants is also a covenant with "every living creature that is with you" (9:10, 12, 15). In the New Testament, we are assured that although two sparrows are sold for as little as a penny, yet "not one of them will fall to the ground without your Father's will" (Matt. 10:29). Truly, "His eye is on the sparrow."

In view of God's well-documented concern for his creatures other than man, perhaps we should support the local branch of the Society for the Prevention of Cruelty to Animals not for humanitarian reasons alone, but on biblical grounds as well. And the annual Service of the Blessing of Pets conducted by certain clerics, hitherto widely regarded as a bit eccentric, may have more support in Scripture than many of us have been willing to concede.

7:17 – 24 *The flood continued. . . . The waters prevailed. . . . And the waters prevailed so mightily. . . .* The narratives of the flood, interwoven as they appear to be, continue, emphasizing its magnitude, its scope, its height, and its depth. It is a description of the reign of death. "Everything on the dry land in whose nostrils was the breath of life died. He blotted out every living thing that was upon the face of the ground, man and animals and creeping things and birds of the air; they were blotted out from the earth." This is a scene of complete devastation.

These words reflect one aspect of God's attitude to human sin: its just penalty is death.

8:1 – 19 *But God remembered Noah and all the beasts and all the cattle that were with him in the ark. . . .* The rain ceased, the winds came, the waters receded, and the ark touched down on Mount Ararat. Noah released a raven (an "unclean" creature) to test the elements. That the raven did not return was a hopeful sign, but far from conclusive. Later he set a dove free, and it came back to him: the time for the evacuation of the ark had not yet arrived. Seven days later he repeated the experiment, and the dove returned bearing an olive leaf. So far, so good; it was only a matter of time until all the creatures could be released from the ark. A week later Noah sent the dove out for the third time and it did not return: the earth was once again habitable.

At a word from God, Noah and his family once more set their feet on dry ground. They bring with them the birds and animals and creeping things that had been their guests for the duration of the flood. Their lives had been spared, and the commandment restored: "that they may breed abundantly on the earth, and be fruitful and multiply upon the earth."

This depicts a second aspect of God's attitude to man's sin: life is the unmerited gift of a merciful God.

65

8:20 – 22 *Then Noah built an altar to the LORD.* . . . Noah, knowing that he and his family no more deserved to be rescued from annihilation by the flood than others of his evil generation, prepared offerings unto the Lord. He "took of every clean animal and of every clean bird, and offered burnt offerings on the altar." Why did he do this, and why at this particular time? From our point of view it might seem more natural to have made the offering before the flood, perhaps in an attempt to placate God's anger and win his favor. But we may learn from Noah's example that our God is not to be "bought off." Noah had already "found favor in the eyes of the LORD" (6:8), and accordingly had not been required to forfeit his life as the penalty for his sin. Preparing animals for sacrifice is an open confession of his guilt. When he destroys the animals and sheds their blood, he is renouncing them for his own use and gratefully acknowledging God's forgiveness. It is for this reason that the Lord found the smell of burning flesh to be a "pleasing odor." It is in the light of Noah's action that God reveals his intention of entering into a covenant with his creature (vv. 21–22).

9:1 – 7 *And God blessed Noah and his sons and said to them, "Be fruitful and multiply, and fill the earth. . . ."* As the human race makes a fresh start in the person of Noah and his family, God's command is much the same as that given to Adam before him. The circumstances, however, are quite different. The command was first given after creation and before the Fall, and God was then addressing himself to innocence. In speaking to Noah this is not the case. Nevertheless God will accept man on these terms, and provide him with an ordered universe and an abundance of the necessities of life. The conduct of the fallen creature will necessarily be circumscribed by precepts and regulations; and man will now be subject to the rule of law. Without these provisions the life of man on earth would be one of perpetual chaos and strife (see Rom. 13).

As Neil puts it, this "is not the world as the Creator intended it to be but . . . a grey world of second-bests, a world where compromise and self-interest are involved in every action. . . . A world of tarnished men who are only prevented from destroying each other by fear of retribution."[5]

The killing and eating of animals is now permitted: "Every

moving thing that lives shall be food for you." Consequently, "the fear of you and the dread of you shall be upon every beast of the earth, and upon every bird of the air, and upon everything that creeps on the ground and all the fish of the sea; into your hand they are delivered." Nevertheless, this wildlife does not belong to man; they and the whole earth can belong only to God. The obvious sense of the phrase "into your hand" is "into your care." Thus, what is required of man is that he exercise his dominion over the nonhuman creatures responsibly. "A righteous man has regard for the life of his beast, but the mercy of the wicked is cruel" (Prov. 12:10).

The prohibition against eating meat which has not been drained of blood arises from the belief that the life of the creature resides in or is identical with its blood. This principle becomes central to all legislation pertaining to animal sacrifices in Israel (see Lev. 7:27; 17:14).* Richardson states: "Such ideas may seem to us to be crude and even superstitious, but unless we try sympathetically to understand them we shall never appreciate the richness of the biblical symbolism of blood—blood-shed: life out-poured—atonement and Christian Eucharist."[6]

Animals may now be killed for man's sustenance and their flesh (though not their blood) may be consumed. However, man may not be killed; not because the life of man is sacred in itself (as in humanism), and not because of a "divine spark" in man (real or imagined), but because God made man in his own image. And the penalty for murder is death. This is the sole exception to the rule that human life may not be forfeited.

9:8–17 *Then God said to Noah and to his sons with him. . . .* The covenant which God has had in mind ("said in his heart," 8:21) is now introduced and established, not only with Noah but with his descendants and with every living creature. Its content and purpose is preservation; its origin and motivation is grace. It will last "for all future generations." Never again will a flood of such proportions as to destroy the earth be released. The

---

*It is also the basis of Jewish dietary law governing what may and may not be eaten today by the practising Jew. Certain meats, prepared in prescribed ways, may be consumed; others are forbidden. Those which are acceptable are known as "kosher"; that is, prepared in accordance with Jewish ceremonial law.

covenant is irreversible: regardless of what may transpire in the history of mankind, God's promise will be kept. The sign of this covenant is the rainbow, which man can see and from which he can take hope, and which God will see and "remember" (v. 15). So begins an era of God's forbearance. Vischer comments: "All the time since the flood is at every moment a respite of grace."[7] It is a time of God's patience when the evil that is done, though rebuked and pardoned, remains unpunished until the coming of the "Lamb of God, who takes away the sin of the world" (John 1:29).

9:18–28 *The sons of Noah who went forth from the ark were Shem, Ham, and Japheth. Ham was the father of Canaan. . . .* Clearly, we are to understand these words as signifying the new beginning of humanity: "from these the whole world was peopled."

Throughout its entire length the Old Testament does not present the reader with a galaxy of "heroes," nor does it encourage us to engage in hero worship. Even the great men of the Bible are shown with their limitations and weaknesses, and the incident of Noah's drunkenness may be a case in point. If Noah drank the wine with the intention of becoming intoxicated, we may regard his conduct as reprehensible. But there is, in this instance, another possibility. If the statement that "Noah was the first tiller of the soil" means that he was also the first to plant a vineyard, and therefore that he was unaware of the qualities of the fermented grape, the resulting intoxication could have been entirely innocent.

In either case, the emphasis in the story is on the actions of Ham, and their consequences. Ham saw his father lying naked in his tent. Instead of quietly covering him and out of respect for his father keeping the incident to himself, he told his two brothers. We may assume that Ham was certain he had a good story to tell on the "old man," and perhaps he told it with some glee. However, he paid dearly for his indiscretion. Upon waking from his stupor and realizing what had taken place, Noah cursed the children of Ham, blessed Shem, and spoke favorably of Japheth.

With these words the story of the flood comes to a close.

CHAPTER NINE

A Parable of Man's Attitude to His Own Sin

11:1– 2 *Now the whole earth had one language and few words.* . . . In taking up the story of the tower of Babel here, we are temporarily setting aside the dispersion of the people into nations recorded in Genesis 10. At the beginning of Genesis 11, mankind is united.* This unity consists in their being the people of one God, in their having been given one language, and in their proximity to one another. As the population increased, some "migrated from the east" and settled on a plain in the land of Shinar. "The land of Shinar is Babylonia, and the plain is the Tigris-Euphrates Valley."[1]

11:3 *Come, let us make bricks, and burn them thoroughly.* . . . Our narrator tells us of a new discovery: the people "had brick for stone, and bitumen for mortar." This development was the occasion, but not the cause, of man's folly. Like all of mankind's subsequent discoveries, developments, and inventions— electricity, dynamite, radio, television, nuclear fission—this one, too, had great potential for good. Permanent shelters could be made, buildings erected, and cities developed. Man's command of the natural forces bearing on his environment has been strengthened and enhanced. Discoveries, inventions, and techniques are in themselves quite neutral: they lead neither

*Chapters 10 and 11:10-32 are taken up in the next section of this chapter. We study the tower of Babel ahead of Genesis 10 because of the break in chronological sequence created by chapters 10 and 11. (See the explanation in the next section.)

to that which is good nor to that which is evil, neither to salvation nor to perdition. Yet the possibilities for good and evil
which are inherent in any new discovery are almost limitless.

11:4 *Then they said, "Come, let us build ourselves a city, and
a tower with its top in the heavens, and let us make a name for
ourselves, lest we be scattered abroad upon the face of the
whole earth."* Surely there is nothing sinful about building a
city, and even a tower. We read that Cain built a city (4:17),
and we hear about the great city of Nineveh (10:12) without
a word of criticism or condemnation. Modern excavations have
yielded the remains of many towers, called *ziggurats,* in the
area of ancient Babylon. Studies show they were religious
rather than secular buildings, topped by sanctuaries and altars.
All of this seems quite wholesome and innocent at Babel—
even commendable—until we are told why the people wanted
to do it. They wanted a tower which would reach to heaven,
a name for themselves, and unity in their midst.

This catalogue of ambitions shows quite clearly man's attitude to his own sin: it is not a serious matter, and it presents
no barrier to achieving his proper destiny by himself. He will
get to heaven on his own initiative and by virtue of his own
efforts. What is wrong with the building of this city and the
erection of this tower? The answer is to be found in the motives
which prompt it. These people want to make a city which will
be a symbol and a guarantee of a unity of their own making,
quite apart from God. They want a tower which, reaching to
heaven, will provide ready access to the kingdom of God—in
short, a salvation which is the product of their own hands.

The whole enterprise is an exercise in self-glorification, in
which the people aspire, as in Genesis 3:5, to be as God—
plotting and devising their own destiny, finding among themselves a unity in which God has no part, and making a "name"
for themselves in preference to the name which he has already
given them. This undertaking is wrong because it is a departure
from grace; or, better, it is a denial of grace and an affirmation
of the validity of man's own works. In addition to being wrong,
all of this is also so unnecessary and so pointless: the people
are already one, and have only to claim it, to confess it, and
to declare it. They are one in being God's people. They already

have a name—God's name, the name of the Lord upon whom they and their ancestors called (4:26). We are reminded of Proverbs 18:10, "The name of the LORD is a strong tower; the righteous man runs into it and is safe," and from Psalm 61:3, "For thou art my refuge, a strong tower against the enemy."

Vischer comments: "To the biblical narrator, and to the biblical prophets who are to follow him, the tower of Babel is more than an ancient event; in it they see a parable of world history."[2] The story of the building of the tower is the pattern of mankind's arrogance down through the centuries to the present day. It is not an incident which took place once only, and upon which we may look back with good-natured nostalgia. There is no need to feel nostalgic about mankind's arrogance; it is very much with us today. Vischer adds: "The conditions and resources for unifying mankind and mastering fate by men were perhaps never so propitious as [they are] today . . . yet how impotent is our generation to solve the simplest problems of life and economics!"[3] This story is thus an enduring indictment of all peoples, societies, and civilizations, whether ancient or modern, which seek to improve their cause without reference to, and in denial of, the will of God. A proposal such as building the tower of Babel, in which the Creator is unseated and dethroned, and his place usurped by the creature, obviously cannot be tolerated.

11:5 – 6 *And the LORD came down to see the city and the tower, which the sons of men had built. And the LORD said. . . .* God will not make a hasty judgment from a great distance. He comes down to see at first hand what has taken place. Once again he proves himself to be solicitous for his creature's well-being—judging if necessary, helpful if needed. What he finds, however, is far from reassuring. Mankind has scorned God's grace and has held in contempt the abundant provisions made for him. "Behold, they are one people, and they have all one language; and this is only the beginning of what they will do; and nothing that they propose to do will now be impossible for them." This may be paraphrased as follows: "If this is what they have done now, there is no telling what they may try next." We may recall in this connection Jesus' words to those following him on the way to the cross, "If they do this when

71

the wood is green, what will happen when it is dry?'' (Luke 23:31). God is saying that if those building Babel are allowed to pursue the wrongheaded course they have chosen, things can only get worse. If only for his own sake, man must be prevented from achieving his self-centered ends and fulfilling his presumptuous ambitions. Otherwise he will quite naturally and inescapably move from dilemma to disaster and from disaster to eventual doom. In this critical situation, recourse to persuasion is out of the question; preventive measures must be taken.

11:7 – 9 *Come, let us go down, and there confuse their language, that they may not understand one another's speech.* . . . The people of the earth are no longer to be a people of one language; and the unity which this common language made possible is to be forfeited. Men will no longer be able to understand one another. Their existence as one people in community is thereby destroyed, and all is in confusion. Of necessity "they left off building the city," and the people were dispersed "over the face of all the earth." Our narrator makes it clear that this scattering of the people is God's work. It is his preventive measure. It is his gracious act whereby man's willfulness will at no future time threaten the existence of the human race.

It is important to recognize that throughout the early chapters of Genesis God's judgments are in every case tempered with mercy. In chapter 3 the penalty for disobedience is death, but the hand of death is stayed; expulsion from the garden (to place man beyond reach of the tree of life) is substituted. After Cain murders his brother Abel, he is banished from the presence of God, but his life is not only spared but protected (chapter 4). When God saw that "the wickedness of man was great upon the earth" and that "the earth was filled with violence," he "determined to make an end of all flesh" (chapter 6), but he also commissioned Noah to build an ark for the saving of mankind.

What we may learn from these chapters is that God's judgment of man, severe though it may be, is always mingled with his mercy. It is never purely condemnatory. Indeed, as in this story, God's anger is frequently shown to be the vehicle of his grace. As a result of God's intervention, the tower which was to have been a guarantee of the people's salvation becomes instead a stunted monument to their folly. Similarly, the city which was intended to be the symbol of their illicit unity was never completed. But the people themselves survived. "And from there the LORD scattered them abroad over the face of all the earth."

* * *

10:1–32 *These are the generations of the sons of Noah, Shem, Ham, and Japheth. . . .* In proceeding from the flood to the tower of Babel, we have momentarily passed over Genesis 10, a genealogy from Noah to Abraham (Abram). This was done to defer for a few pages the problem of the unusual and somewhat awkward sequence that results when we move from 10:32 to 11:1. We read in 10:32 that "the nations spread abroad on the earth after the flood," but at 11:1, the beginning of the story of Babel, we read, "Now the whole earth had one language and few words." So at the outset of this new section we move back in time to the time prior to 10:32.

It appears that in Genesis 10 and 11 we have two accounts of the dispersion of the people of God—somewhat after the fashion of the two stories of creation and the two (interwoven) narratives of the flood. In each of these three pairs of stories, the two accounts complement one another, and there is much to be learned from studying both.

The purpose of the genealogy in Genesis 10 is obviously to give an account of the development of the descendants of Noah into a "world family," or family of nations. That this is God's doing is evident from Deuteronomy 32:8—"When the Most High gave to the nations their inheritance, when he separated the sons of men, he fixed the bounds of the peoples," and from Acts 17:26—"He made from one every nation of men to live on the face of all the earth, having determined allotted periods and the boundaries of their habitation."

So the peoples of the earth are dispersed and go their separate ways in families and nations. Humanity is still one, but it is now differentiated according to lands, languages, and national loyalties (vv. 5, 20, and 31).

We can see that there are significant differences between

the account of the dispersion of God's people here in Genesis 10 and that given in the story of Babel. In chapter 10 we read of a relocation—a natural process that takes place over a considerable period of time. There is no hint of compulsion here, and no suggestion that this was a divine judgment. In the story of Babel, however, the people were *compelled* to leave; they were expelled from their common dwellingplace. God is displeased with his people at Babel, and "confusion" and "scattering" result.

Genesis 10 may also be regarded as a transition between the focus on a single line of descent from Adam to Noah, set forth in the genealogy in Genesis 5, and the context of a world family for the telling of the history of salvation which begins in Genesis 12. In chapter 5 it is almost as though the people who make up the families of the ten generations from Adam to Noah are the only people in the world. Yet before this point there are indications of the existence of others; but they are not named and have no place in the central theme of the narrative. One such person was Cain's wife (4:17), of whom nothing further is known. In chapter 5 there is more evidence that there are other people in the world, for we are told that Adam's descendants "had other sons and daughters." We are aware of their existence, but they play no part in the story the Bible is intent on telling. We never hear of them again.

What we experience in reading chapter 10 is a little different. The narrator of this chapter is concerned not only with the descendants of the three sons of Noah, but also with the nations which they are said to have founded and to which they give their names. We could characterize this chapter as broad and comprehensive.

A football game on television can serve to illustrate the difference between the genealogies in chapters 5 and 10. As play is about to begin, the camera is focused on the ball. We are watching the center's hand on the ball, and are but dimly aware of the crowd. We watch the ball because that is where the "action" is. When the ball is snapped, the camera shifts immediately to a wide-angle picture so that we can follow the play. And in this new picture perhaps we catch a glimpse of the spectators—a nameless, nonparticipating crowd.

Something like this is taking place in the genealogies in

chapters 5 and 10. In chapter 5 (and the material in chapters 1–4 and 6–9) there is no mention of peoples or nations. We are dimly aware of their existence, but our attention is riveted on a single line of descent, because that is where the action (God's action) is taking place. All else is of secondary interest. In chapter 10, however, the picture switches from a focus on a single line of descent to the wide-angle view of peoples of many nations and languages.

We can say, therefore, that the aim of the narrator in Genesis 10 is to demonstrate that God's purpose for the world he has created embraces all nations. This story of God's purpose for all nations begins with his call of Abraham in Genesis 12.

11:10 – 32 *These are the descendants of Shem*. . . . This record is in some respects similar to the genealogy in chapter 10, but it serves a different purpose. Here the focus of our camera narrows once again, and we find ourselves following a single line of descent once more—a line from Shem to Abraham, the man God called into his service and with whom he made his covenant on behalf of mankind.

CHAPTER TEN

Abraham and the Nations

Genesis 1–11, which has been the focus of our study thus far in this volume, is a prelude, in pictorial form, to God's covenant history with Israel and all mankind. With the appearance of the name of Abraham (Abram) on the pages of Scripture, the Bible is launched on its two-thousand-year story of the covenant of God with him—and, through him, with all mankind. It takes the form of the history of a particular and newly created people, the Israelites, within and among the peoples of the world, yet distinct and even separated from them. It is the history of salvation within the compass of the history of civilizations, but differentiated from it. This new people is a new creation of God (12:2) by virtue of his election and blessing of Abraham and his family. The Israelites find their sole *raison d'être* in God's calling and covenanting with them, for they are to be uniquely his people: "It is he that made us, and we are his; we are his people, and the sheep of his pasture" (Ps. 100:3).

So begins the history of a people who are singular in the sight of God. They will bear God's (as yet unspecified) promise and blessing to "all the families of the earth" (12:4), including, of course, those which are now "scattered . . . abroad over the face of all the earth" (11:9). In this connection we may recall the words of the prophet: "I will not execute my fierce anger, . . . for I am God and not man, the Holy One in your midst, and I will not come to destroy" (Hos. 11:9).

It is implicit in the calling of Abraham that he is not called for himself alone, nor yet for only his descendants, for "in you all the families of the earth shall be blessed" (alternate reading, RSV). A corresponding text and assurance in the New Testament is from the words of Simeon when he saw the child Jesus: "Mine eyes have seen thy salvation . . . a light for revelation to the Gentiles, and for glory to thy people Israel" (Luke 2:30–32).

Thus, in the person of Abraham, God begins his majestic work of the redemption of the world; and the story the Old Testament has to tell is the story of this new people. It begins with the election of Abraham and continues with Isaac rather than Ishmael, Jacob rather than Esau, and Judah among the twelve sons of Jacob, in order that all may know that their inheritance is of God's grace alone, not of merit or standing among men.

This theme of election and rejection, which begins with Abel and Cain, is continued throughout the Bible—Moses and Pharaoh, David and Saul, Israel and the nations—until election *and* rejection are manifested in Jesus Christ. For he is the Elect of God: "And when Jesus was baptized, he went up immediately from the water, and behold the heavens were opened and he saw the Spirit of God descending like a dove, and alighting on him; and lo, a voice from heaven, saying, 'This is my beloved Son, with whom I am well pleased' " (Matt. 3:16–17; see also Luke 3:21–22). He is also the Rejected of God: "And about the ninth hour Jesus cried with a loud voice, 'Eli, Eli, lama sabachthani?' that is, 'My God, my God, why hast thou forsaken me?' " (Matt. 27:46; see also Mark 15:34). So Jesus of Nazareth, Son of God and Son of Man, lives and dies "the righteous for the unrighteous" (1 Peter 3:18; KJV: "the just for the unjust"). He is at once the elected and the rejected Man in whom all mankind has been rejected in order to be elected as a new creature in him.*

Accordingly, it is important to Matthew (1:1–16) to assert the Abrahamic origin of the Man Jesus through the Davidic line of descent as confirmation of the claim that in him the promise made to Abraham is fulfilled, namely, that in Jesus,

---

*It is interesting and instructive to observe that Jesus, in many of his parables, pursues the theme of election by God's free grace. Examples are: the publican and the Pharisee (Luke 18:9–14); the prodigal son and the elder brother (Luke 15:11–32); the Samaritan and the priest and the Levite (Luke 10:25–37); and "both good and bad," originally ignored, and the invited guests in the parable of the marriage feast (Matt. 22:1–10).

"who is called Christ," "all the families of the earth are blessed."

During the centuries between the covenant with Abraham and the birth of Jesus, God was Israel's God, and Israel was his people. Their uniqueness among the nations consisted solely in this relationship with God. Alternately unfaithful and repentant, disobedient and contrite, the people of the promise were at no time forsaken by the God who made it. But this "Mighty One of Israel" was no mere tribal deity, concerned for one people only. By the mouth of the prophets Israel was constantly reminded of the meaning of its election: "Behold my servant, whom I uphold, my chosen, in whom my soul delights; I have put my Spirit upon him, he will bring forth justice to the nations. . . . I have given you as a covenant to the people, a light to the nations" (Isa. 42:1, 6). It is expressly *for the nations* that Israel is called to be the servant of the Most High God.

At the birth of Jesus the heralding angel spoke to this theme of God's concern for all people and also comforted the shepherds with the words, "Be not afraid; for behold, I bring you good news of a great joy *which shall come to all the people*" (Luke 2:10). And by the Spirit of God Simeon cites Isaiah 49:6 in grateful recognition that the infant before him is the promised Savior of the world.

Jesus himself put forward the truth that God's love extends to all people in the synagogue at Nazareth, when he made public announcement of his mission. After reading Isaiah 61:1-2, he said: "Today this scripture has been fulfilled in your hearing" (Luke 4:21). His listeners were overjoyed and wondered at his "gracious words"; or at least until he, with two examples from the Old Testament (the widow of Zarephath and Naaman the Syrian), showed them that Israel was never intended to be the sole beneficiary of God's mercy. Then they tried to kill him.

Despite the fact that Jesus knew his mission to be to all people, it is evident from the Gospel records that he conceived his *personal ministry* to be primarily to the Jews. When he called and commissioned his disciples, he charged them, "Go nowhere among the Gentiles, and enter no town of the Samaritans, but go rather to the lost sheep of the house of Israel"

(Matt. 10:5–6). There were exceptions, however: the centurion's servant (Luke 7:1–10); the centurion at the cross (Matt. 27:54); the Samaritan woman at Jacob's well (John 4:7–28); and the Canaanite woman from the region of Tyre and Sidon (Matt. 15:21–28) are examples.

During Jesus' ministry on earth, estimated to have been between one-and-a-half and three years long, many of those who witnessed his signs (miracles) and heard him preach believed on his name. The mission of the twelve was followed by the mission of the seventy (Luke 10:1–20). And so the little company of believers grew. Then, suddenly, tragedy struck. Jesus was seized, arrested, tried, found innocent—and crucified. His stunned and bewildered disciples could only say, "We had hoped that he was the one to redeem Israel" (Luke 24:21).

It is thoroughly understandable that the disciples, in their confusion and deep despair, should think of themselves (and their immediate company) first. What would now become of Israel? they wondered. But God had something far more comprehensive on his mind and heart than just Israel, namely, What would become of the *world*? "For God so loved the *world* that he gave his only Son. . . . [He] sent the Son into the world, not to condemn the world, but that the *world* might be saved through him" (John 3:16–17). What, in short, would become of those families and people of whom we were told that the Lord confused their language, denied their aspirations for a name, dampened their hopes for a unity other than that which he would give them, and scattered them over the face of the earth (Gen. 11:1–9)?

All three synoptic Gospels conclude with the stories of the crucifixion, the resurrection, and the postresurrection appearances of Jesus. And then follows his command to preach to all nations: "Go therefore and make disciples of all nations . . . (Matthew). "Go into all the world and preach the gospel to the whole creation" (Mark; see footnote in RSV). "Repentance and forgiveness of sins should be preached in his name to all nations. . . . But stay in the city, until you are clothed with power from on high" (Luke).

In the opening verses of the Book of the Acts the great commission is restated, as well as the exhortation to the disciples not to leave Jerusalem before being baptized with the

Holy Spirit. They "with one accord devoted themselves to prayer" (v. 14); and, seeking a replacement for Judas, drew Matthias.

As the disciples waited in Jerusalem for the gift of the Spirit, the season of one of the three annual festivals of Israel was approaching. Pentecost, or the Feast of Weeks, was a harvest festival celebrating "the first fruits of wheat harvest, and the feast of ingathering at the year's end" (Exod. 34:22).

In John 12:24 Jesus states, "Unless a grain of wheat falls into the earth and dies, it remains alone; but if it dies, it bears much fruit." And in Luke 10:2, when sending out the seventy, he says, "The harvest is plentiful, but the laborers are few; pray therefore the Lord of the harvest to send out laborers into his harvest." In view of what Jesus says in these two places, it may not be entirely fanciful to believe that the Spirit was sent on the day of Pentecost at least in part because of the rich symbolism embodied in this day. Certainly, the divine Seed had fallen into the earth and died, and was about to bear much fruit.

The inception of the church—that is, of a new people of God—is told in terms of a "sound . . . from heaven like the rush of a mighty wind," of "tongues as of fire," of people being "filled with the Holy Spirit," and speaking "in other tongues." As others gathered round, they were bewildered, because "each one heard them speaking in his own language" (Acts 1). These people in Jerusalem who heard Christ's followers speaking in tongues were Jews of the dispersion—from Europe, Asia, and Africa; and each heard the disciples speak in the language native to his own district.

When reading the account of Pentecost in the Book of the Acts, it is difficult to overlook its similarity, in reverse, to the story of Babel. As William Neil observes, "The common language at Pentecost . . . is in effect the Tower of Babel turned upside down."[1] On the plain in the land of Shinar the people had but one language, which all understood. They lived in community with one another and with God, on whose name they called. Overtaken with pride, seeking a unity of their own apart from God and a name for themselves other than God's name, they set out to build two monuments: one to their common identity—a city; and one to their self-sufficiency—a tower.

God countered this effrontery by confounding their language, thus making communication impossible, and by expelling them from the plain.

At Pentecost, events moved in precisely the opposite direction. The people assembled in Jerusalem for the feast had come from widely disparate areas of three continents bordering on the Mediterranean Sea. They spoke different languages and dialects. But on this day, each one heard the disciples and their company "speaking in his own language" (Acts 2:6). What they heard was a "telling in our own tongues the mighty works of God" (v. 11).

The significance of the delirium experienced at Pentecost was not immediately evident. Some thought it was evidence of intoxication (v. 13). But Peter, addressing the crowd, put the matter in its proper perspective. This was not drunkenness; it was the outpouring of the Holy Spirit as foretold by the prophet Joel (2:28–32).

For confirmation of Peter's claim that this was the Spirit, let us consider the outcome of this miraculous visitation. We are told that the disciples and those who waited with them for baptism by the Holy Spirit numbered "in all about a hundred and twenty" (1:15). At the conclusion of Peter's address we read, "There were added that day about three thousand souls" (2:41). Subsequently, at worship in the temple and in fellowship in their homes, "the Lord added to their number day by day those who were being saved" (v. 47).

The gathering of the church is presented by Luke as a new creation of God by the power of his Spirit. It is a new people, such that those who belong to Christ are truly children of Abraham according to the promise made to him (see Gal. 3:29). Among them there are no distinctions of race, color, sex, or station in life. "*All* who call upon the name of the LORD shall be delivered" (Joel 2:32). The phrase "children of Abraham" takes on new meaning in the incarnation, death, and resurrection of Jesus Christ: it is a term used of all those whose sins are forgiven through faith in him (see Gal. 3:7, 14). In the gospel as proclaimed by Peter at Pentecost—and since his time by the whole church—"there *cannot* be Greek and Jew, circumcised and uncircumcised, barbarian, Scythian, slave, free man, but Christ is all, and in all" (Col. 3:11).

The dispersion and scattering at Babel is countermanded and nullified by the event of Pentecost, in which peace is proclaimed to those who were afar off and to those who were near. Through Christ, "we both have access in one Spirit to the Father" (Eph. 2:17). Hence the second verse of a well-known hymn of the church:

> Elect from every nation,
>   Yet one o'er all the earth,
> Her charter of salvation,
>   One Lord, one faith, one birth;
> One holy name she blesses,
>   Partakes one holy food,
> And to one hope she presses,
>   With every grace endued.
>   —Samuel John Stone

Throughout his letters Paul proclaims, attests, and extols the unity of the church.* The body of Christ is one, born of one Spirit, so that "you are no longer strangers and sojourners, but you are fellow citizens with the saints and members of the household of God" (Eph. 2:19). And again, "There is one body and one Spirit, . . . one Lord, one faith, one baptism, one God and Father of us all, who is above all and through all and in all" (Eph. 4:4–5).

The church, the "new Israel," is called into existence at Pentecost. To what end, and for what purpose? The disciples were commissioned by Jesus to "go into all the world and preach the gospel to the whole creation" (Mark 16:15). Later (1 Pet. 2:9), Peter reminded the church of its calling: "You are a chosen race, a royal priesthood, a holy nation, God's own people." And of its purpose: "that you may declare the wonderful deeds of him who called you out of darkness into his marvelous light."

And, even today, this is your mandate and mine.

---

*See Romans 12:4–5; 1 Corinthians 10:17; 12:12–13, 20; Galatians 3:28.

A Personal Postscript

The word *evolution* does not occur anywhere in the foregoing chapters of this book. The reason for this must surely be apparent: the subject is never mentioned, even indirectly, in the text of Scripture. However, in view of the current debate between creationists and evolutionists, particularly as it pertains to school curricula, a few brief comments may be in order.

First, if creation is what Scripture says it is—namely, creation out of nothing—then there is a fatal flaw in the arguments put forward by both parties. Those who believe that "in the beginning God created the heavens and the earth" are not taking their sources seriously when they appeal to science (legitimate or otherwise) to bolster their faith in the Word of God. No science, of whatever kind, is capable of dealing with Nothing: science and the scientific method require data, information, and substance in order to be truly scientific. The legitimate sciences (biology, astronomy, archaeology, paleontology, etc.) suffer a similar delimitation. They cannot, in the nature of the case, bridge the gap between nonexistence and existence, between nonbeing and being. We may learn much from them of the forces and nature of change, and how things came to be the way they are. But insofar as they may feel obliged to deny creation in order to affirm evolution (or other), we must call upon them to halt.

Second, it is not clear that creation and evolution are mutually exclusive in their claims to validity, except (as noted) when science presumes to be dealing with the primeval origin of the universe. There are literally millions of convinced Christian men and women, including the present writer, to whom the evolutionary premise is quite inoffensive as an explanation of change.

It is little wonder that the issue is no nearer being resolved today than when it started—and the court cases began. Both parties to the debate are arguing from the same mind-set, namely, fundamentalism. On both sides the argument depends heavily on a dogma of human inerrancy. Why should each listen to what the other has to say? Both appear to believe that they have exclusive access to the truth by reason of their "infallible" sources.

Biblical fundamentalism and its handmaiden, the doctrine of the literal inerrancy of Scripture, have been around for only about 130 years, give or take a few. In the history of Christian thought it is therefore a comparative newcomer. Certainly, none of the ancients (one thinks, for example, of Origen of Alexandria and the great St. Augustine of Hippo) nor the Reformers of the sixteenth century could be placed in this category. All of them had the utmost reverence for the inspiration and authority of Scripture; but they stopped short of biblical idolatry.

This school of thought is very largely of North American origin, and arose as a reaction to the historical and literary examination of the text of Scripture taking place in Europe. Such analysis was widely believed to undermine the biblical message. At about the same time came Darwin's *Origin of the Species* (1859).

In the face of such challenges there appeared, at the time, only one thing to do: deny the validity of the findings of the scholars and Darwin by affirming the literal and historical infallibility of the Bible. (It is interesting to note, without comment, that the doctrine of the infallibility of the Pope was promulgated in 1870.)

Dyed-in-the-wool evolutionists are beginning to make the same mistake, quoting Suzuki, Sagan, and Einstein with the same lack of reserve that the opposition exhibits in quoting from the Bible. Accordingly, they have developed a kind of scientific fundamentalism which ignores the possibility of error both in the scientific method and in the scientists themselves.

Evolution is certainly a theory, and it may very well be a fact. I do not claim to know. There is apparently a great deal of evidence in support of it. But who knows whether tomorrow, or the next day, the same mass of observed data may not be considered more congenial to a somewhat different hypothesis?

So what is the present position? On the one hand, we are being asked to accept without reservation the findings of scientific research as though it were "gospel truth." And, on the other, science (the mortal enemy!) is being dragooned (as in Arkansas) into verifying the Word of God!

I dare to hope that this little volume may make a small contribution to the resolution of a problem which is tearing both the church and society apart.

Endnotes

Chapter 2

[1]Dietrich Bonhoeffer, *Creation and Fall,* trans. J. C. Fletcher (London: SCM, 1959), pp. 9–10. Probably the most brilliant German theologian since Martin Luther, Bonhoeffer was put to death by the Nazis for his opposition to the Hitler regime. His influence on Christian thought has been out of all proportion to his comparatively few published works.

[2]Quoted by Logan, *In the Beginning God* (Atlanta: John Knox, 1961), p. 33.

[3]Quoted by Peter Mosher, *The Globe and Mail,* Science section, Toronto, November 19, 1979.

[4]Walter Luthi, *St. John's Gospel* (Edinburgh: Oliver and Boyd, 1960), p. 2.

[5]D. T. Niles, *In the Beginning* (London: Lutterworth, 1958), p. 13.

Chapter 4

[1]Bonhoeffer, *Creation and Fall*, p. 15.

[2]Karl Barth, *Church Dogmatics,* 4 vols. (Edinburgh: T. & T. Clark, 1958), vol. 3/1, p. 120. Karl Barth (1886–1968), a Swiss theologian and the author of this prodigious dogmatics and of many shorter works, is widely regarded as one of the most influential Protestant theologians of the twentieth century.

[3]Origen of Alexandria, *On First Principles,* trans. G. W. Butterworth (New York: Harper & Row, Harper Torchbooks, 1966), book 4, chap. 3. Origen of Alexandria (c. A.D. 185–c. 254) was one of the Ante-Nicene fathers of the church. Jerome called him "the greatest teacher of the church after the apostles."

[4]St. Augustine, *The City of God,* trans. John Heale (London: J. M. Dent & Sons, 1947), Everyman's Library, vol. 1, book 11, chap. 6. St. Augustine (A.D. 354–430) was ordained a presbyter in 391, and consecrated Bishop of Hippo in 395. He wrote his famous *Confessions* and many other treatises and commentaries.

[5]John Calvin (1509–1564) was the author of the celebrated *Institutes of the Christian Religion*, and of commentaries on more than sixty books of the Bible. He was a leader of the Reformation in Europe.

[6]Martin Luther, *Luther on Genesis*, trans. Henry Cole (Edinburgh: T. & T. Clark, 1858), p. 115. Luther (1483–1546), the central figure in the Reformation movement in Germany, wrote voluminously on biblical and theological subjects, including many commentaries.

[7]Barth, *Church Dogmatics*, vol. 3/1, p. 126.

[8]Bonhoeffer, *Creation and Fall*, p. 25.

[9]Derek Kidner, *Genesis*, Tyndale Old Testament Commentaries (Downers Grove, Ill.: Inter-Varsity, 1977), pp. 54–58.

[10]Alan Richardson, *Genesis I–XI*, Torch Bible Commentaries (London: SCM, 1953), p. 51.

[11]Charles T. Fritsch, *The Book of Genesis*, The Layman's Bible Commentary (Atlanta: John Knox, 1959), p. 23. (Note: the quotation is correct as it stands; but "geological" is probably intended where "geographical" appears.)

[12]Bonhoeffer, *Creation and Fall*, p. 25.

[13]*Ibid.*, p. 26.

[14]Barth, *Church Dogmatics*, vol. 3/1, p. 182.

[15]Kidner, *Genesis*, p. 53.

Chapter 5

[1]Bonhoeffer, *Creation and Fall*, p. 47.

Chapter 6

[1]Bonhoeffer, *Creation and Fall*, p. 83.

[2]Wilhelm Vischer, *The Witness of the Old Testament to Christ*, trans. A. B. Crabtree (London: Lutterworth, 1949), vol. 1, p. 64.

[3]*Ibid.*, p. 65.

[4]Bonhoeffer, *Creation and Fall*, p. 93.

[5]Thomas Gray, *Elegy Written in a Country Churchyard*.

Chapter 7

[1]Richardson, *Genesis I–XI*, p. 86.

[2]Barth, *Church Dogmatics*, vol. 3/2, pp. 635–36.

Chapter 8

[1]William Neil, *Harper's Bible Commentary* (New York: Harper & Row, paperback ed., 1975), p. 29.

[2]Richardson, *Genesis I–XI,* p. 97.
[3]Neil, *Harper's Bible Commentary,* pp. 31–32.
[4]Barth, *Church Dogmatics,* vol. 2/1, p. 413.
[5]Neil, *Harper's Bible Commentary,* p. 33.
[6]Richardson, *Genesis I–XI,* p. 108.
[7]Vischer, *The Witness to Christ,* pp. 101–102.

Chapter 9

[1]*The Interpreter's Bible* (New York & Nashville: Abingdon-Cokesbury, 1952), vol. 1, pp. 563–64.
[2]Vischer, *The Witness to Christ,* p. 110.
[3]*Ibid.*

Chapter 10

[1]Neil, *Harper's Bible Commentary,* p. 422.